FOR A FUN-LOVING GUY OR GAL WHO HAS EVERYTHING

A Funny Book

(Adults Only)

Team Golfwell and Bruce Miller

i

For a Fun-Loving Guy or Gal Who Has Everything, A Funny Book (Adults Only), Copyright ©2023 Team Golfwell and Bruce Miller. All rights reserved as to the collective work only and no part of this publication may be reproduced, distributed, or transmitted in any form or by any means, including photocopying, recording, or any other electronic, mechanical, or other methods.

The jokes are fictitious and any similarity to actual events or locales or persons, living or dead, is entirely coincidental. Cover by Queen Graphics. Cover picture from Shutterstock and other pictures, and illustrations are from Creative Commons unless otherwise indicated.

ISBN: 978-1-99-104828-8 (Ingram Spark paperback B&W)

ISBN: 978-1-99-104830-1 (Ingram Spark paperback color)

ISBN 978-1-99-104829-5 (Ingram Spark hardback B&W)

ISBN: 978-1-99-104831-8 (Ingram Spark hardback color)

ISBN: 9798393353001 (Amazon paperback)

ISBN: (Amazon hardback)

ISBN: (Amazon paperback color)

ISBN: (Amazon hardback color)

"You may tell a joke or funny story which reaches someone's heart and inspire them, and who knows what they might do because of the laughs you bring them."

- Erin Morgenstern, The Night Circus

Introduction

"Laughter is the best medicine. Go ahead and give it a try. Turn the corners of your mouth up into a smile and then give a laugh, even if it feels a little forced.

"Once you've had your chuckle, take stock of how you're feeling. Are your muscles a little less tense? Do you feel more relaxed or buoyant? That's the natural wonder of laughing at work. It will brighten anyone's mood!" -- The Mayo Clinic. [1]

This is a delightful and enjoyable book filled with good-natured adult humor, hilarious trivia, crazy facts, interesting world records, unusual and funny events, and stories, and much more!

It makes a great and memorable gift for the Holidays, birthdays, Father's or Mother's Day, in-laws, friends, co-workers, or anyone!

Perfect for,

- Sharing with friends.
- Funny conversation starters.
- Humor on a wide variety of subjects.
- Funny one-liners and hilarious long stories.
- Keep it on the nightstand, read it while traveling, or anytime!

It will brighten anyone's mood! Laughter is something we all love!

Turn your or someone else's day around with humor. Enjoy!

Screwdriver. I asked my wife to bring me a screwdriver.

She replied, flat head, Phillips, or Vodka?

That brought a tear to my eye, as at that moment I knew I married the right one. She's absolutely priceless!

Engineers. The mind of an engineer is different as they see the world and everything in it as a system. They see structures that others don't see and know designs and understand trade-offs.

For example, many years ago, a doctor, a lawyer and an engineer are arrested during the French Revolution for the crime of being rich and are sent to the guillotine.

The executioner brings the doctor up the steps first.

"How do you wish to die Monsieur?"

"I wish to die with honor" replies the doctor. This means that he goes into the guillotine headfirst with no blindfold, so he can face the blade that will end his life. So, in he goes, no blindfold, face up.

The executioner pulls the cord, the blade falls... and stops halfway down. The executioner being a superstitious man exclaims, "Monsieur, God must want you to live. We cannot execute you. You are free to go."

Next comes the lawyer. "How do you wish to die Monsieur?"

"I wish to die with honor" replies the lawyer. So, in he goes, no blindfold, face up.

The executioner pulls the cord, the blade falls... and again stops halfway down.

"Monsieur, God must want you to live. We cannot execute you. You are free to go," says the executioner.

Next comes the engineer. "How do you wish to die Monsieur?" The engineer, being no fool, replies, "I too wish to die with honor." And so, in he goes, no blindfold, face up.

The executioner reaches for the cord, unsure what will happen next when the engineer says, "Wait! I see the problem."

A baby is coming! My husband frantically calls the hospital ER and shouts, "My wife is going into labor!"

Hospital ER: "Is this her first child?"

Husband: "No, this is her husband!"

Scotsman splurge. A Scotsman and his wife walk past a fancy new restaurant and his wife says, "Did you smell that food? It smells absolutely incredible!"

Being a kind-hearted Scotsman, he decides *What the hell, I'll treat her.*

So, they walk past it again.

How Many? How many times does the average person laugh in a day?

A. Amazingly, the average 4-year-old laughs 300 times a day while the average 40-year-old laughs only 4 times a day. [2]

Quiz Question. You can sneeze in your sleep. True or False?

(Answer on p. 182)

Today is really unusual. "Today is a most unusual day because we have never experienced it before. We will never live it again. It is the only day we have." **-- William Arthur Ward,** Author

Aging. "We can't stop the aging process, but it would be wonderful if we could put ourselves in the dryer for ten minutes, then come out wrinkle-free and three sizes smaller." -- Anon.

Danger. Funny, those road signs: "Caution - Watch for children!"

I mean, how dangerous can a child be?   -- Anon.

Things haven't changed much. Over 2,000 years ago, Socrates said, "Children now love luxury too much and have bad manners, and contempt for authority. They disrespect elders and love to talk instead of exercising."

The doctor and the old man. A doctor buys one of the best cars on the market, a brand-new Ferrari. It is also one of the most expensive cars in the world, and it cost him $500,000.

The doctor takes it out for a spin and stops at a red light. An old man on a moped, looking about one hundred years old, pulls up next to him.

The old man looks over at the sleek shiny car and asks, "What kind of car ya got there, sonny?"

The doctor replies, "A Ferrari – it's brand-new and it cost a half- million dollars!"

"That's a lot of money," says the old man. "Why does it cost so much?"

"Because this car can do up to 250 miles an hour!" states the doctor proudly.

The moped driver asks, "Mind if I take a look inside?"

"No problem," replies the doctor.

The old man pokes his head in the window and looks around.

Then, sitting back on his moped, the old man says, "That's a pretty nice car, all right, but I'll stick with my moped!"

Just then the light changes, so the doctor decides to show the old man just what his car can do. He floors it, and within seconds, the speedometer reads 150 mph.

Suddenly, he notices a dot in his rear-view mirror - what it could be...and suddenly...WHHHOOOOOOSSSSSHHH! Something whips by him going much faster!

"What on earth could be going faster than my Ferrari?" the doctor asks himself.

He floors the accelerator and takes the Ferrari up to 175 mph.

Then, up ahead of him, he sees that it's the old man on the moped!

Amazed that the moped could pass his Ferrari, he gives it more gas and passes the moped at 210 mph.

WHOOOOOOOSHHHHH!

He's feeling pretty good until he looks in his mirror and sees the old man gaining on him AGAIN!

Astounded by the speed of this old guy, he floors the gas pedal and takes the Ferrari to 250 mph!

Not ten seconds later, he sees the moped bearing down on him again! The Ferrari is flat out, and there's nothing he can do!

Suddenly, the moped plows into the back of his Ferrari, demolishing the rear end. The doctor stops and jumps out and unbelievably, the old man is still alive.

He runs up to the mangled old man and says, "Oh my gosh! Is there anything I can do for you?"

The old man whispers, "Unhook my suspenders from your side mirror."

Choices. Two engineering students were talking on campus. One had a brand-new bike. The other student asked him where he got it.

"I was here on campus when a beautiful co-ed rode up to me with this bike. Then she put the bike down and stripped naked and said, "Have it your way and take whatever you want."

The first engineering student said, "Great decision. Her clothes wouldn't have fit you."

A few fun conversation starters.

- What was the last thing that you did for fun?
- What's the weirdest thing that a guest has done at your house?
- What is the most fun thing to do at an amusement park?
- What's your best "my office or coworkers are crazy" story?

Happy birthday. "My father drank so heavily, when he blew on the birthday cake, he lit the candles." – **Les Dawson**

Fishing. Joe was speeding in his brand-new Porsche on a desert road when suddenly he was passed in a flash by a motorcyclist. He continued for a half-mile when he was pulled over by the police for speeding.

The officer handed Joe the citation, received his signature and was about to walk away when Joe asked, "Officer, I know I was speeding, but I don't think it's fair – did you see that motorcycle fly by me? Why did you give me the ticket and not him?"

"Ever go a-fishin'?" the policeman asked.

"Yeah, sure," Joe replied.

The officer grinned, "Did you ever catch 'em all?"

Expressway to heaven. Church officials discussed the nuisance of cell phones going off during church services. They decided to put a sign at the entrance which read:

"It is unlikely the Good Lord will call you on your mobile while you are here, so please turn it off before entering our Church.

If you want to contact God, do so on your own in a quiet place where no one will disturb you.

If you want to see God, just text him when you are driving a car."

Honest people. True story. Last year after my golf round, I stopped to get gas and discovered my back pocket was torn, and my wallet must have fallen out and was gone. I went back to the course but no luck.

A week after, I received a package from Milwaukee, Wisconsin. No name on it, only a return address. Not enough info to contact the sender before opening it and this happened at the time Anthrax in mail packages were all over the news. So, I was reluctant to open it.

After a short time, my curiosity finally got the best of me. Lo and behold, my wallet! Everything was intact ($400+ and all the credit cards and gift cards).

I thanked my good Samaritan with a box of new golf balls Pro V1x and a round when he is passing through again. We became friends on FB.

The moral: There are still good people in this world, especially golfers!

Full-service counseling. A husband and wife are sitting in the office of a marriage counselor after 20 years of marriage.

The wife is going on and on. "He goes bowling too much, drinks too much, eats too much, he's always gone, he's lazy, he neglects me, he doesn't listen to anything I say…"

Not saying a word, the counselor gets up and goes around the desk, and passionately takes the woman in his arms, kissing her repeatedly. The woman is stunned and silent.

The counselor turns to the husband and says, "What I just did is what your wife needs at least three times a week. Do you get the picture? Can you do that?"

Husband is thinking, then says, "I can bring her in on every Wednesday and Friday, but on the other days, I've got bowling."

Ever want to get away from it all? Mongolia has the world's lowest population density on the planet. The horse population outnumbers its human population.

It is a vast landlocked country from Russia in the north to China in the south. There are parts where you can go for days without seeing another person. In some regions, it's possible to go days without coming across another person. The topography consists of mountainous terrains, rolling plateaus, grasslands, and arid desert steppes. If you want to escape, this might be the place for you but be sure to dress warmly as the average temperature is -4 C to -8 C.

New truck. A sixteen-year-old boy came home with a brand-new Ford truck.

His parents look at the truck and ask, "Where did you get that truck?!"

"I bought it today," he says. "With what money?" says his mother. They knew what a new truck cost.

"Well," he says, "this one cost me just fifteen dollars."

The father looks at him like he's crazy. "Who would sell a truck like that for fifteen dollars?" he says.

"It was the lady up the street," says the boy. "I don't know her name - they just moved in. She saw me ride past on my bike and asked me if I wanted to buy her F150 for fifteen dollars."

"Oh, my Goodness!" says the mother. "Maybe she's mentally ill or has Alzheimer's something. John, you better go see what's going on."

The boy's father walks up the street to the house where the lady lives and finds her out in the yard calmly planting flowers. He introduces himself as the father of the boy to whom she had sold a new Ford truck for fifteen dollars and asks to know why she did it.

"Well," she says, "Two days ago my husband left on a business trip. Yesterday I got a phone call from his boss and found out that he really ran off to Hawaii with his secretary and doesn't intend to come back."

"Oh, my goodness, I'm so sorry," the father says. "But what does that have to do with my son and your truck?"

"Well, this morning he called and told me he was stranded because he got robbed of his wallet with all his credit cards and cash. He told me to sell his new truck and send him the money. So, I did."

Getting Stronger Over the Years? It is good to try and stay fit. One man bragged when he was 20 years old, his manhood was as hard as an "iron bar." But now being 65, he finds he can bend it and it's not as hard as an iron bar anymore.

His friend replied he could bend an iron bar over his manhood when he was young.

But now, being much older, he can't do it since his wrists aren't strong enough.

Eyebrows. I told my girlfriend she drew her eyebrows too high. She seemed surprised.

Unexpected understatement. "I had pro offers from the Detroit Lions and Green Bay Packers, who were hard up for linemen in those days. If I had gone into professional football the name Jerry Ford might have been a household word today."

-- President Gerald Ford

Forgetting things? In case you were wondering, it is illegal to forget your wife's birthday in Samoa. You may just get a warning from the policeman, but it definitely is against the law.

Instead of a warning, you may get a fine plus some serious explaining to do when you get home! [3]

Oh, never mind. True story. A Detroit man watched on as police were showing school children their new car computer which located felons.

The Detroit man stepped up and asked more about how it worked.

The police asked him for his license and ran it through the computer and then arrested him for being wanted for an armed robbery in St. Louis two years earlier.

Operation. A man was involved in a terrible car crash and was rushed to the hospital. Just before the operation, the surgeon popped in to see him.

"I have some good news and some bad news," says the surgeon. "The bad news is that I have to remove your right arm!"

"Oh God no!" cries the man "My sporting days are over... Please Doc, what's the good news?"

"The good news is, I have another one to replace it with, but it's a woman's arm and I'll need your permission before I go ahead with the transplant."

"Go for it doc," says the man, "as long as I can play sports or even play golf again."

The operation went well and a year later the man was out on the golf course when he bumped into the surgeon.

"Hi, how's the new arm?" asks the surgeon.

"Just great," says the businessman. "I'm playing the best golf of my life. My new arm has a much finer touch, and my putting has really improved."

"That's great," said the surgeon.

"Not only that," continued the golfer, "my handwriting has improved. I've learned how to sew my own clothes and I've even taken up painting landscapes in watercolors."

"That's unbelievable!" said the surgeon, "I'm so glad to hear the transplant was such a great success.

Are you having any side effects?"

"Well, just two," said the man, "I have trouble parallel parking and every time I get an erection, I get a headache."

Female NFL. "The reason women don't play football is that eleven of them would never wear the same outfit in public."

   -- Phyllis Diller

You get what you pay for. TV host Graham Norton said, "A good rule to remember for life is that when it comes to plastic surgery and sushi, never be attracted by a bargain."

Sad, but as I get older, I think differently. After a long day on the golf course, I stopped in at Hooter's to see some friends and have some hot wings and beer.

After being there for a while, one of my friends asked me which waitress I would like to be stuck in an elevator with.

I told them "The one who knows how to fix elevators. I'm old, I'm tired, and I pee a lot."

So how cold was it? The coldest place on Earth. The valley of Oymyakon in Yakutia known as "The Pole of Cold" is in northeast Russia. The temperature goes as low as -70°C (-94 F).

It's home to 500 Siberian people engaged in reindeer herding, hunting, and fishing. Tourism is just starting up if you can stand the cold.

Heaven or hell? While walking down the street one day a female official who recently won the election for head of state is tragically hit by a truck and dies.

Her soul arrives in heaven and is met by St. Peter at the entrance.

"Welcome to Heaven," says St. Peter. "Before you settle in, it seems there is a problem. We seldom see a high official around these parts, you see, so we're not sure what to do with you."

"No problem, just let me in," says the lady.

"Well, I would like to, but I have orders from higher up. What we will do is have you spend one day in Hell and one in Heaven. Then you can choose where to spend eternity."

"Really, I've made up my mind. I want to be in Heaven," says the head of state.

"I'm sorry but we have our rules." And with that, St. Peter escorts her to the elevator and she goes down, down, down to Hell. The doors open and she finds herself in the middle of a green golf course. In the distance is a club and standing in front of it are all her friends and other politicians who had collaborated with her, everyone is very happy and in evening dress. They run to greet her, hug her, and reminisce about the good times they had while getting rich at the expense of the people. They play a friendly game of golf and then dine on lobster and caviar.

Also present is the Devil, who really is a very friendly guy who has a fun time dancing and telling jokes. They are having such an enjoyable time that, before she realizes it, it is time to go. Everyone gives her a big hug and waves while the elevator rises.

The elevator goes up, up, up and the door reopens on Heaven where St. Peter is waiting for her. "Now it's time to visit Heaven." So, 24 hours pass with the head of state joining a group of contented souls moving from cloud to cloud, playing the harp and singing.

They have a fun time and, before she realizes it, the 24 hours have gone by and St. Peter returns. "Well then, you've spent a day in Hell and another in Heaven. Now choose your eternity."

She reflects for a minute, then the head of state answers: "Well, I would never have said it, I mean Heaven has been delightful, but I think I would be better off in Hell."

So, Saint Peter escorts her to the elevator and she goes down, down, down to Hell. Now the doors of the elevator open and she is in the middle of a barren land covered with waste and garbage. She sees all her friends, dressed in rags, picking up the trash and putting it in black bags.

The Devil comes over to her and lays his arm on her neck. "I don't understand," stammers the head of state. "Yesterday I was here and there was a golf course and club and we ate lobster and caviar and danced and had an exciting time. Now there is a wasteland full of garbage and my friends look miserable.

The Devil looks at her, smiles and says, "Yesterday we were campaigning. Today you voted for us!"

Keys locked inside. True story. When my wife and I arrived at a car dealership to pick up our car after a service, we were told the keys had been locked in it. We went to the service department and found a mechanic working feverishly to unlock the driver's side door.

As I watched from the passenger side, I instinctively tried the door handle and discovered that it was unlocked.

"Hey," I announced to the technician, "It's open!"

His reply was, "I know. I already did that side."

Lineman v. Backs. Marvin Ventner, the football coach, was asked about his secret of evaluating his recruits.

"'Well," he answered, "It's easy. I take 'em out in the woods and make 'em run. The ones that run round the trees, I make into running backs. The ones that run straight into the trees, I turn into linemen."

Job Interview.

Interviewer: What's the reason for this 4-year gap in your resume?

Applicant: That's when I went to Yale.

Interviewer: That's impressive! You are hired!

Applicant: Thank you. I really needed this yob.

Just in case you want to know. We all are familiar with the old saying, "When you gotta go you gotta go." So, if you and your pregnant wife happen to be in the UK, you might want to know that it is illegal for a pregnant woman to relieve herself in a policeman's helmet in the UK. [4]

Some countries are so picky and proper. What happened to the policeman's motto, "Deeds not words?" Is it now, "Pee and you get words?"

Snow White was returning from town to the cottage in the forest where she lived with the seven dwarfs. In the distance she could see smoke, then as she got nearer, she realized that their cottage had burnt down.

Frantically, Snow White searched the forest for the dwarfs, then she heard a lone voice saying, "Bears will win the next Superbowl! Somalia will win the FIFA World Cup!"

On hearing this chant, Snow White gave a little sigh of relief as she knew that at least Dopey was safe.

Negotiating. A lonely and wealthy woman walks into a bar and sees an incredibly handsome and attractive man sitting at the bar.

She slides onto the stool next to him and orders a drink from the bartender.

As the bartender is working on her drink she turns to the man and says, "You're very handsome - would you have sex with me for $100,000?"

At first, the man is shocked and taken aback but starts mulling over the dollar figure in his head, and then smiles and responds, "Sure."

The woman then says, "How about $20 bucks?"

The man's attitude turns to outrage, and he responds, "What the hell? ... Where did the one hundred grand go? Do you think I am a professional gigolo?"

And the woman calmly replies, "We've already established that, now we're just dickering over price."

If you think your life is boring. There is a Village in Scotland called Dull in Perthshire. Dull has only one street of houses and a church. The crazy thing is that the town is twinned with a town in the US named Boring, and a town in Australia called Bland. Those residents have a profound sense of humor in our view!

Word choice. I decided to stop calling the bathroom "John" and renamed it "Jim". I feel so much better saying I went to the Jim this morning.

Mountain pun. Honestly, this may be a hot take, but mountains aren't funny.

They're hill areas.

Exercise for Seniors. Begin by standing on a comfortable surface, where you have plenty of room on each side.

With a 5 lb. potato bag in each hand, extend your arms straight out from your sides and hold them there as long as you can. Try to reach a full minute, and then relax.

Each day you'll find that you can hold this position for just a bit longer.

After a couple of weeks, move up to 10-lb. potato bags. Then try 50-lb. potato bags and eventually try to get to where you can lift a 100-lb. potato bag in each hand and hold your arms straight for more than a full minute. (I'm at this level).

After you feel confident at that level, put a potato in each bag.

Caribou. Why was the caribou wearing a disguise?

A. He wanted to remain anonymoose.

Fitness. Patient: Doctor, my problem with obesity runs in my family.

Doctor: No, the problem with your family is that no one runs.

Impossible. It is impossible to hold your nose and hum at the same time. Try it!

Q. Should I really have to touch my toes?

A. If God wanted me to touch my toes, He would've put them on my knees.

Accents. Why do I have to press one for English when you're just going to transfer me to someone I can't understand anyway?

Caution grim humor. A man who'd just died is delivered to a local mortuary wearing an expensive, expertly tailored black suit...

The female mortician asks the deceased's wife how she would like the body dressed. She points out that the man looks good in the black suit he is already wearing.

The widow, however, says that she always thought her husband looked his best in blue and that she wanted him in a blue suit.

She gives the Blonde mortician a blank check and says, "I don't care what it costs, but have my husband in a blue suit for the viewing."

The woman returns the next day for the wake. To her delight, she finds her husband dressed in a gorgeous blue suit with a subtle chalk stripe; the suit fits him perfectly...

She says to the mortician, "Whatever this cost, I'm very satisfied... You did an excellent job and I'm incredibly grateful. How much did you spend?"

To her astonishment, the blonde mortician presents her with the blank zeroed-out invoice. "There's no charge," she says.

"No, really, I must compensate you for the cost of that exquisite blue suit!" she says.

"Honestly," the blonde says, "It cost nothing. You see, a deceased gentleman of about your husband's size was brought in shortly after you left yesterday, and he was wearing an attractive blue suit. I asked his wife if she minded him going to his grave wearing a black suit instead, and she said it made no difference as long as he looked nice."

"So, I just switched the heads."

Saving up. A small tourist hotel was all abuzz about an afternoon wedding where an elderly groom who was 80 and the bride was only 23.

The groom looked feeble, and the feeling was that the wedding night might kill him because his bride was a healthy, vivacious young woman.

But lo and behold the next morning, the bride came down the main staircase slowly, step by step, hanging onto the banister for dear life.

She finally managed to get to the counter of the little shop in the hotel. The clerk looked really concerned, "Whatever happened to you, honey? You look like you've been wrestling an alligator!"

The bride groaned, hung onto the counter and managed to speak, "Ohhhh God! He told me he'd been saving up for 65 years and I thought he meant his money!"

Old is new again. Almost one hundred years ago, Will Rogers is reported to have said, "Everything is changing. People take comedians seriously and people take politicians as a joke."

Amazing how even more true that has become in the present day.

Champagne? What Benedictine monk invented champagne?

A. Dom Pierre Pérignon

Won the dance contest. I got wasted at my sister's wedding. I won the dance contest, caught the garter, caught the bouquet, got engaged, and got into a fight as I crossed the dance floor just trying to get another drink.

Dramatic send-off. A heart surgeon passed away and his family had a very fancy funeral. A family donated a ten-foot heart made up of roses which were placed behind the casket.

When the service finished, the casket was solemnly and slowly wheeled through the heart made of roses and into his final resting place. The heart then automatically closed in on the casket sealing the casket forever.

One of the mourners couldn't help but break out in laughter. Then he quickly recovered and said, "I'm deeply sorry. That beautiful heart sealing made me think of my own funeral ceremony. You see, I'm a gynecologist."

Another mourner, a proctologist, left suddenly.

Choice of words. The Smiths were unable to conceive children and decided to use a surrogate father to start their family. On the day the proxy father was to arrive, Mr. Smith kissed his wife goodbye and said, "Well, I'm off now. The man should be here soon."

Half an hour later, just by chance, a door-to-door baby photographer happened to ring the doorbell, hoping to make a sale. "Good morning, Ma'am', he said, 'I've come to..."

"Oh, no need to explain,' Mrs. Smith cut in, embarrassed, 'I've been expecting you."

"Have you really?" said the photographer. "Well, that's good. Did you know babies are my specialty?"

'Well, that's what my husband and I had hoped. Please come in and have a seat.

After a moment she asked, blushing, "Well, where do we start?"

"Leave everything to me. I usually try two in the bathtub, one on the couch, and perhaps a couple on the bed. And sometimes the living room floor is fun. You can really spread out there."

"Bathtub, living room floor? No wonder it didn't work out for Harry and me!"

"Well, Ma'am, none of us can guarantee a good one every time. But if we try several unusual positions and I shoot from six or seven angles, I'm sure you'll be pleased with the results."

"My, that's a lot!" gasped Mrs. Smith.

"Ma'am, in my line of work a man must take his time. I'd love to be in and out in five minutes, but I'm sure you'd be disappointed with that."

"Don't I know it," said Mrs. Smith quietly.

The photographer opened his briefcase and pulled out a portfolio of his baby pictures. "This was done on the top of a bus," he said.

"Oh, my God!" Mrs. Smith exclaimed, grasping at her throat.

"And these twins turned out exceptionally well - when you consider their mother was so difficult to work with."

"She was difficult?" asked Mrs. Smith.

"Yes, I'm afraid so. I finally had to take her to the park to get the job done right. People were crowding around four and five deep to get a good look."

"Four and five deep?" said Mrs. Smith, her eyes wide with amazement.

"Yes," the photographer replied. "And for more than three hours, too. The mother was constantly squealing and yelling -

I could hardly concentrate, and when darkness approached, I had to rush my shots. Finally, when the squirrels began nibbling on my equipment, I just had to pack it all in."

Mrs. Smith leaned forward. "Do you mean they actually chewed on your, uh...equipment?"

"It's true, Ma'am, yes. Well, if you're ready, I'll set-up my tripod and we can get to work right away."

"Tripod?"

"Oh yes, Ma'am. I need to use a tripod to rest my Canon on. It's much too big to be held in the hand – it's exceptionally long."

Mrs. Smith fainted.

To avoid tears, stick it in the freezer for 15 minutes. Chilling onions in the freezer for at least 15 minutes before chopping will prevent the acid enzymes from having the usual adverse effects and stop the tears.

Realization. "I have a lot of growing up to do. I realized that the other day inside my blanket living room table fort." – **Zach Galifianakis**

Stairs. "I like an escalator because an escalator can never break. It can only become stairs. There would never be an 'Escalator Temporarily Out of Order' sign, only 'Escalator Temporarily Stairs'." – **Mitch Hedberg**

Coming in second. "If I were an Olympic athlete, I'd rather come in last than win the silver medal.

"You win the gold, you feel good. You win the bronze, you think, 'at least I got something.'

"But you win that silver, that's like, 'Congratulations, you almost won! Of all the losers, you came in first! You're the number one loser! No one lost ahead of you!'" – **Jerry Seinfeld**

Not religious. "We weren't deeply religious. On Hanukkah, my mother had our menorah on a dimmer." – **Richard Lewis**

Thanks Doctor! (Just kidding!) A woman and a baby were in the doctor's examining room, waiting for the Doctor to come in for the baby's first exam.

The Doctor arrived, examined the baby, checked his weight, and seeming a little concerned, asked if the baby was breastfed or bottle-fed.

"Breast-fed," she replied.

"Strip down to your waist," the Doctor said.

She did.

He pinched her nipples, then pressed, kneaded, and rubbed both breasts for a while in a detailed examination. Motioning her to get dressed, he said, "No wonder this baby is underweight, you don't have any milk."

"I know," she said, "I'm his Grandma, but I'm glad I came."

Revenge. "My therapist says I have a preoccupation with vengeance. We'll see about that.'" **– Stewart Francis**

Getting married. Three virgin sisters were all getting married within a short time.

Mom was a bit worried about how their sex life would get started and made them all promise to send a postcard from the honeymoon with a few words on their first impressions of marital sex.

The first girl sent a card from Hawaii two days after the wedding.

The card said nothing but: "Nescafe".

Puzzled at first Mom went to her kitchen and got out the Nescafe jar.

It said: "Great from beginning to end".

Mom blushed but was pleased for her daughter.

The second girl sent the card from the Maldives a week after the wedding and the card read: "Rothmans".

Mom now knew to go straight to her husband's cigarettes to read from the pack: "Super strong King Size".

She was again slightly embarrassed but still happy for her daughter. The third girl departed for her honeymoon in New Zealand.

Mom waited for a week,

Nothing.

Another week went by and still nothing.

A month passed, and still nothing.

A card finally arrived from Auckland which was written with a shaky hand, "Air New Zealand ".

Mom took out her latest travel magazine, flipped through the pages fearing the worst, and finally found the ad for Air NZ which read, "Ten times a day, seven days a week, in all directions."

Signing a cast. "The easiest time to add insult to injury is when you're signing somebody's cast." **– Demetri Martin**

5 o'clock. There should be a truck that drives around the business district at 5 pm as workers go to catch the train home playing bagpipe music so men could come out to the curb and greet it with dollars in their hands, just like an ice cream truck, but only with, you guessed it, scotch and fine cigars!

Darwin was unusual. He may have been one of the greatest minds of all time, but he was unusual. He drew up a pro and con list to help him decide whether he should get married. Not too romantic.

He also was fond of eating unusual animals like owls, ostriches, and pumas.

He had a very cool side though since in his home, Darwin built a slide for his kids instead of having stairs.

By the way, he had 10 kids, but sadly 3 died at birth. The other 7 lived long lives.

Pulled over. "I was in my car driving back from work. A police officer pulled me over and knocked on my window. I said, 'One minute I'm on the phone.'" – **Alan Carr**

Get a loaf of bread. A wife sends a text to her husband, "Honey don't forget to stop at the bakery and buy bread with your girlfriend Valerie."

Husband sends a text back, "Who is Valerie?"

Wife: "Nobody, I just wanted you to answer so I know you got my text."

Husband: "But I'm with Valerie right now! I thought you saw me!"

Wife: "What! Where are you?!"

Husband: "Near the bakery."

Wife: "Wait, I'm coming right now!"

Five minutes later, the wife sends another text. "I'm at the bakery. Where are you!"

Husband: "I'm at work. Now that you're at the bakery, buy the bread. XX."

The Priest and the Rabbi. A priest and a rabbi were sitting next to each other on a train and the priest asked the rabbi if the Jewish faith still prohibits eating pork.

"Yes, we have that belief," the rabbi replied.

"I see. Rabbi, have you ever eaten pork?" The priest asked.

The rabbi paused then said, "Yes, once in my life I ate a ham sandwich." The priest smiled and began reading.

"Does your faith require you to remain celibate?" The rabbi asked the priest.

"Yes, it is an important part of our church and that is required."

"Father, have you ever succumbed to the temptations of the flesh?" The rabbi asked.

The priest paused then said, "Yes, rabbi, on one occasion, I had too much wine and broke my vow and made love to a woman."

The rabbi was silent for several minutes thinking about what the priest just told him, then said, "Beats a f*cking ham sandwich, doesn't it?"

Wilson. "Somebody once told me I treated my smartphone like 'Wilson', the volleyball Tom Hanks turns into a friend when he's stranded on a desert island in that movie 'Castaway.'"

"It's a fair comparison since if you are raising little ones, you feel like you have been stranded on a dessert island and the only connection with the real world is your phone." -- **Rachel Simmons**, author

Girl talk. A good girlfriend will stop you from drinking when you've had too much. Your best friend forever will say, "Bitch, you better drink this 'cause we're not wasting this sh*t."

Avoid eating beans. Florida has a highly unusual law. It is illegal to fart in public places after 6 pm on Thursdays. [5] Talk about difficult laws to enforce!

Imagine if you happen to let one lose, well-informed law-abiding people around you would be pointing at you saying things like, "He did it!" or "There he is!"

Appropriately named. A girl was visiting her blonde friend, who had acquired two new dogs, and asked her what their names were.

The blonde responded by saying that one was named "Rolex" and one was named "Timex".

Her friend said, "Whoever heard of someone naming dogs like that?"

"Helllooooo...!" answered the blonde. "They're watchdogs."

Ethical Issues. An attractive airline flight attendant said, "Captain I'm in love with you. Won't you kiss me, please?"

"No, it would be against my code of ethics," said the captain.

"Please just one kiss?"

"It's completely out of the question," said the captain. "I shouldn't even really be having sex with you."

Tough landing. A small private plane was flying over the Everglades near southwest Florida when suddenly, the engine died. Being miles away from any airport the pilot turned to his wife and said, "Don't worry honey, I'll just land on one of the dozens of golf courses in the area."

To this, his wife replied "What do you mean don't worry? I've seen you play. You'll never hit the fairway."

Slinky. Mechanical engineer Richard James invented the Slinky by accident. In 1943, he was working to devise springs that could keep sensitive ship equipment steady at sea. After accidentally knocking some samples off a shelf, he watched in amazement as they gracefully "walked" down instead of falling. [6]

Say again? A young husband comes home one night, and his wife throws her arms around his neck. "Darling, I have great news - I'm a month overdue. I think we're going to have a baby! The doctor gave me a test today, but until we find out for sure, we can't tell anybody."

The next day, a guy from the electric company rings the doorbell, because the young couple hadn't paid their last bill. "Are you Mrs. Smith? You're a month overdue, you know!"

"How do you know?" stammers the young woman. "Well, ma'am, it's in our files!" says the man from the electric company.

"What are you saying? It is in your files???"

"Absolutely."

"Well, let me talk to my husband about this tonight."

That night, she tells her husband about the visit, and he, mad as a bull, rushes to the electric company offices the first thing the next morning. "What's going on here? You have it on file that my wife is a month overdue? What business is that of yours?" the husband shouts.

"Just calm down," says the clerk, "It's nothing serious. All you have to do is pay us."

"Pay you? And if I refuse?"

"Well, in that case, sir, we'd have no option but to cut yours off."

"And what would my wife do then?" the husband asks.

"I don't know. I guess she'd have to use a candle."

Humbling. "People with a superiority complex may be condescending, smug, or mean to other people who don't agree with them. Whenever you feel like this, take up golf." – Anon.

Quick thinking. A woman was enjoying a good game of golf with her girlfriends. "Oh, no!" she suddenly exclaimed. "Look at the time! I must rush home and fix dinner for my husband! He'll be so pissed if it's not ready on time."

When she got home, she discovered all she had in the fridge was a wilted lettuce leaf, an egg - and a can of cat food.

With no time to go to the supermarket, she opened the can of cat food, stirred in the egg, and garnished it with the lettuce leaf. She greeted her husband warmly when he came home, and then watched in horror as he sat down for his dinner.

To her surprise, he seemed to be enjoying it "Darling, this is the best dinner you've made me in 40 years of marriage! You can make this for me any day?"

Every golf day from then on, the woman made her husband the same dish.

She told her golf partners about it, and they were all horrified.

"You're going to kill him!" they exclaimed. Two months later, her husband died.

The women were sitting around the clubhouse and one of them said, "You killed him "We told you that feeding him that cat food every week would do him in! How can you just sit there so calmly knowing you murdered your husband?"

The wife stoically replied, "I didn't kill him. He fell off the windowsill while he was licking his arse."

Legal search? A Michigan defendant was on trial for possession of illegal substances and raised the defense of being searched without a warrant.

The prosecutor argued that the officers had reasonable cause to search him since there was a bulge in his jacket which could have been a firearm.

The defendant disagreed and testified he was wearing the same jacket in court and took off his jacket and handed it to the judge to show him.

The judge examined the jacket and discovered a packet of cocaine in the jacket. The judge couldn't stop laughing at his discovery and called a short recess.

Faking it. Women fake orgasms to have relationships. Men fake relationships to have orgasms.

Another old one. A big city lawyer was playing a beautiful course and hit his ball out of bounds into the backyard of a private residence. As the golfer was climbing climbed the fence to retrieve it, an elderly man walked out his back door and asked him what he was doing.

The golfer responded, "I sliced my drive, and it went in your yard and now I'm going to retrieve it."

The senior citizen replied. "This is my property, and you are not coming over here."

The indignant lawyer said, "I am one of the best trial attorneys in the U.S. and, if you don't let me get that Pro V1, I'll sue you and take everything you own."

The old man smiled and said, "Apparently, you don't know how we do things here. We settle small disagreements like this with the Three Kick Rule."

The lawyer asked, "What is the Three Kick Rule?"

The old man replied, "Well, first I kick you three times and then you kick me three times, and so on, back and forth, until someone gives up."

The attorney quickly thought about the proposed contest and decided that he could easily take the old codger. He agreed to abide by the local custom.

The old man slowly crossed his yard and walked up to the city feller. His first kick planted the toe of his heavy work boot into the lawyer's shin and dropped him to his knees. His second kick landed square on the man's nose. The barrister was flat on his belly when the senior's third kick to a kidney nearly caused him to give up.

The lawyer says, "My turn now."

The old man says, "Aw, you win, you can have your golf ball."

Intercom. A 777 was coming into New York JFK after a long-haul trip from Frankfurt. The captain looking forward to a break, announced over the intercom, "Ladies and gentlemen we are now making our final approach into JFK, we hope you've enjoyed flying with us and we'll see you again soon, and we hope you have a safe onward journey to your final destination."

Inadvertently leaving the intercom on, he turned to his co-pilot and said, "Well what's up for you this evening?"

"Oh, my wife is at the hotel, Joe, and she's got seats booked for theatre, I don't know which one, what plans do you have?"

The passengers enjoyed hearing this exchange between the pilots.

The captain continued. "Hey, my divorce was finalized last week so I'll be taking a long soak in the bath before ordering dinner in my room. I'm thinking I'll call the pretty new blonde stewardess, Josephine, I think her name is, and take her out for a drink then take her back to my room and give her a good rogering."

The passengers began to cheer, as Josephine scrambled to turn off the intercom and ran up the aisle. She tripped over an old lady's carry-on bag halfway up and fell flat on her face.

The old lady said, "There's no need to hurry my dear, he's got to take a bath first."

Speaks every seven years. A man drives by a monastery every day for years and through the trees sees glimpses of a beautiful and mysterious golf course. He is a golf fanatic and wants to play the course so badly, he decides to stop by.

The elder monks tell him if he joins the monastery he would live there and could play unlimited golf but there is one rule. He must take a vow of silence and is only allowed to speak two words every seven years.

The man's thinking, I just lost my job, my wife left me, and I have to declare bankruptcy, so why not? I'll join the monastery!

After the first seven years, the elders bring him in and ask for his two words. "Greens bad," he says. They nod and send him away.

Seven years pass. They bring him back in and ask for his two words. He clears his throat and says, "Fairways brown."

They nod and send him away.

Seven more years have passed. They bring him in for his two words. "I quit," he says.

"That's not surprising," the elders say, "You've been nothing but a chronic complainer ever since you got here."

What is the flavor? What flavor is Cointreau? A. Orange. By the way, Forbes reported Cointreau wants people to add Cointreau to their Margaritas on May 5th – Cinco de Mayo. [7] What happened to the lime?

What's that name? Two older couples are playing tennis doubles when the conversation turns to their health. The one guy says his arthritis has been flaring up lately. The second older gentleman says, "You should go see my doctor, he's a miracle worker, added ten yards to my drive.

The other guy says, "Great, what's his name?"

The second guy starts scratching his head and says, "Oh geez, I can't recall, let me think, uh.... what's the name of that flower, you know, it's red, they sell them by the dozen?"

45

The first guy says, "Rose?"

The second guy's face lights up and he turns to his wife and says, "Hey Rose, what's the name of my doctor?"

You might have heard this one. Bob left work one Friday evening. But it was payday, so instead of going home, he stayed out the entire weekend partying with his mates and spending his entire wages.

When he finally appeared at home on Sunday night, he was confronted by his angry wife and was barraged for nearly two hours with a tirade befitting his actions.

Finally, his wife stopped the nagging and said to him, "How would you like it if you didn't see me for two or three days?"

He replied, "That would be fine with me."

Monday went by and he didn't see his wife.

Tuesday and Wednesday came and went with the same results.

But on Thursday, the swelling went down just enough that he could see her a little out of the corner of his left eye.

Tossing dwarfs. Are you breaking the law if you toss a dwarf?

A. It is illegal in Florida to toss a dwarf. [8] Good to know just in case things get out of hand at a party in Florida!

The traffic true test. Before you marry someone sit in traffic with them for two hours.

46

Innocent. A man stood outside his house after a bitter divorce and noticed a crate of beer bottles. He angrily looked down at the crate and took out an empty bottle and smashed it against the wall shouting, "You are the reason I don't have a wife!"

He picked up a second bottle and smashed it against the wall shouting, "You are the reason I don't have children!"

He picked up a third bottle, and smashed it against the wall shouting, "You are the reason I don't have a job."

He picked up the fourth bottle. It was a perfectly good bottle of beer with the cap still on it. He said to the bottle, "YOU STAND ASIDE, I KNOW YOU WERE NOT INVOLVED!"

No thank you. A woman was running down the hall with only her hospital gown on before she was about to be operated on. A guard stopped her and asked her what was going on.

"Well, the nurse was saying, 'This will be a very simple operation. Don't worry so much about it even though it's the first time.'"

The guard said, "The nurse was just trying to make you relax and not be nervous about the operation."

"But she wasn't saying that to me. She was saying that to the young doctor!"

Can I have a cookie? An elderly man lay dying in his bed. In death's agony, he suddenly smelled the aroma of his favorite chocolate chip cookies wafting up the stairs. He gathered his remaining strength and lifted himself from the bed. Leaning against the wall, he slowly made his way out of the bedroom, and with even greater effort forced himself down the stairs, gripping the railing with both hands, he crawled down the stairs.

With labored breath, he leaned against the doorframe, gazing into the kitchen. Were it not for death's agony, he would have thought himself already in heaven: there, spread out upon waxed paper on the kitchen table were literally hundreds of his favorite chocolate chip cookies. Was it heaven? Or was it one final act of heroic love from his devoted wife, seeing to it that he left this world a happy man?

Mustering one great final effort, he threw himself toward the table, landing on his knees in a rumpled posture. His parched lips parted: the wondrous taste of the cookie was already in his mouth, seemingly bringing him back to life.

The aged and withered hand trembled on its way to a cookie at the edge of the table, when it was suddenly smacked with a spatula by his wife.

"Stay out of those," she said, "they're for the funeral."

Okaaay... I was at the airport, checking in at the gate when an airport employee asked, "Has anyone put anything in your baggage without your knowledge?"

"If anyone put something in my luggage, how would I know?"

He smiled knowingly and nodded, "That's why we ask."

Small difference. What's the small difference between a Captain of an airliner and God?

A. God doesn't think He's a captain of an airliner.

Double-edged. "An optimist usually thinks we are in the best of all possible worlds. Ironically, the pessimist also believes this but fears this is true."

-- James Branch Cabell

Senior flight attendants. Three senior flight attendants were discussing memory problems in the galley during a flight.

The first one said, "Sometimes I find myself standing in front of the refrigerator holding a dinner and I can't for the life of me remember whether I need to put it away or serve it."

The second one said, "Yes, I know what you mean. Sometimes I'll be halfway back in the plane aisle and can't remember whether I was on my way up or on my way down."

The third senior flight attendant knocked her hand on the table and rather smugly said, "Well, I'm glad I don't have those problems! Knock on wood!"

While she was knocking her knuckles on the table, she announced, "That must be someone at the door. I'll get it!"

Choices. An older couple went on a cruise. At the end of the first day, the wife's hearing aid battery went dead.

They looked at the gift shop and different stores on the boat and couldn't find a battery to fit. They got back to their room and the man realized they had mistakenly been given a room with bunk beds. So, he asked her if she wanted top or bottom.

She couldn't hear and just said "What?"

He repeated and she still couldn't hear him. So, he yelled and pointed his finger "UP OR DOWN?!"

She grabbed him and threw him around the room giving him the wildest sex they had ever had.

The next day came and went and still were not able to find the battery. So, the same thing happened, and she could hear him, so he yelled "UP OR DOWN?!"

Again, she threw him around having the wildest sex ever. This continued each night of the cruise.

Finally, they got back home and got a battery to fit the hearing aid. They got home and ready for bed that night. He thought to himself it worked on the cruise might as well try it again, and he yells "UP OR DOWN?!"

She smacks him and says, "I thought you were saying f#ck or drown!"

What it takes. Men, if you want to have a woman to love you, you should always tell her you love her, and think about her. Buy her gifts now and then and give her flowers. Always listen to her when she speaks and always respect her.

Women, if you want a man to love you, have nothing on under your coat and carry a 12-pack of beer.

Lose yourself. "Lose yourself in generous service and every day can be a most unusual day, a triumphant day, an abundantly rewarding day!" **-- William Arthur Ward**

Just waiting. A woman decides to surprise her husband with a brand-new luxury wardrobe. While he's at work she goes to IKEA and finds a beautiful wardrobe, buys it, and returns home. Reading the instructions, she easily assembles the marvelous piece of furniture.

Then, as she stood admiring her work, a bus passed by the window and the whole wardrobe fell apart.

Stunned, the woman assembles the wardrobe again, making sure she follows the instructions exactly. When she finishes all of it looked perfect, but a few minutes later a bus passes, and again the wardrobe falls to pieces!

At this point, the woman has had enough, and calls customer support to explain the wardrobe she bought collapsed whenever a bus passed. The man on the other end insists that they provide any service necessary for the proper installation of their furniture, and sends over the very carpenter who designed the wardrobe to help. The carpenter watches as the woman assembles, seemingly perfectly, the wardrobe. And yet, as the next bus passes it falls to pieces again!

Determined to figure out the issue, the carpenter helps her rebuild the wardrobe and enters inside to see exactly what happens when a bus passes. Suddenly the woman's husband bursts through the front door, demanding to know why the neighbors had texted him saying a strange man had been in their house for hours.

Surging through the house he throws open the doors until he comes across the new wardrobe. He opens the door to the wardrobe to reveal the carpenter inside and demands to know what he was doing there!

Shocked, the carpenter says, "Would you believe me if I said I'm waiting for the bus?"

True Story. Please indulge me a bit. So, I am at Walmart self-scanning and bagging my almost $300 worth of groceries while an employee monitors my activities from her "podium". And then this happened.

Her - Why are you double-bagging all of your groceries?

Me - Excuse me?

Her - You are wasting our bags.

Me - If you don't like the way I'm bagging the groceries, feel free to come on over here and bag them yourself.

Her - That's not my job!

Me - Okay, then I will bag my groceries how I please if that's alright with you.

Her - Why are you using two bags?

Me - Because the bags are weak, and I don't want the handles to break or the bottoms to rip out.

Her - Well, that's because you are putting too much stuff in the bag. If you took half of that stuff out and put it in a different bag, then you wouldn't need to double bag.

(10 seconds of me just staring at her)

Me - So you want me to split these items in half and put half of them in a different bag so that I don't have to double bag?

Her - Exactly.

Me - So I would still be using two bags to hold the same number of items.

Her - No because you wouldn't be double-bagging.

(Me pressing two fingers to my left eye to make it stop twitching.)

Me - Okay. So here I have a jug of milk and a bottle of juice double bagged. If I take the milk out and remove the double bagging and just put the milk in the single bag and the juice in that single bag, I'm still using two bags for these two items.

Her - No, because you are not double-bagging them so it's not the same number of bags.

(Me looking around at about 10 other customers who at this point are enjoying the show.)

Me - Is this like that Common Core math stuff I keep hearing about?

Her - Never mind. You just don't get it.

And with that, she went back to her little podium so she could continue texting or playing games on her phone or whatever it was she was doing before she decided to come over and critique my bagging skills.

Dichotomy. "If you write a story about failures, and the book doesn't sell very well. Is the book a success?" -- **Jerry Seinfeld**

Double-edged sword. The good part of losing is that it's only temporary. The bad part about winning is that it's only temporary.

Another true story. We had to have the garage door repaired. The repairman told us that one of our problems was that we did not have a 'large' enough motor on the opener.

I thought for a minute and said that we had the largest one made at that time, a one-half (1/2) horsepower.

He shook his head and said, "You need 1/4 horsepower."

I responded that 1/2 was larger than 1/4 and he said, "NOOO, it's not. Four is larger than two."

We haven't used that repairman since.

No job for you.

Interviewer: "What do you think is your greatest weakness?"

Man: "My honesty."

Interviewer: "But, I think honesty isn't a weakness."

Man: "I don't give a f*ck what you think."

Transferred to Texas. A priest from Ireland was transferred to Texas, and Father O'Malley rose from his bed on the first morning in the Lone Star State. It was a fine spring day in his new West Texas mission parish.

He walked to the window of his bedroom to get a deep breath of the beautiful day outside. He then noticed there was a jackass lying dead in the middle of his front lawn.

He promptly called the local police station. The conversation went like this:

"Good morning. This is Sergeant Jones. How might I help you?"

"And the best of the day to yerself. This is Father O'Malley at St. Ann 's Catholic Church. There's a jackass lying dead in me front lawn and would ye be so kind as to send a couple o'yer lads to take care of the matter?"

Sergeant Jones, considering himself to be quite a wit and recognizing the Irish accent, thought he would have a little fun with the good father, replied, "Well now Father, it was always my impression that you people took care of the last rites!"

There was dead silence on the line for a long moment... Father O'Malley then replied, "Aye,'tis certainly true, but we are also obliged to notify the next of kin first, which is the reason for me call."

Long airport departure lines. Being at the back of a long line at the Departure check-in, an ill-mannered and irate customer butted through and said, "Look here, I can't wait in this line! Not me! You know who I am?"

The departure clerk used an old joke by announcing to everyone in the long line, "May I have your attention, please? There is a customer here who does not know who he is. Does anyone here know who this person is?"

The irate customer said, "F*ck you!"

The departure clerk replied, "I'm very sorry, sir, but you have to wait in line for that too."

Banned in Indonesia. What was banned in Indonesia for "stimulating passion?"

(Answer on p. 182)

The inquiring minds of kids. A study reports children from the ages of 2 to 5 ask from two hundred to three hundred questions during an average day.

So, by the time a child is 5 years old, the child has asked approximately forty thousand questions! -- **Warren Berger**, Author, "A More Beautiful Question"

Last request. A man went to the Doctor and the doctor told him he had only 24 hours to live.

He goes home to tell his wife and after they both had a long cry over it, he asked her if she would have sex with him since he only had 24 hours to live.

"Of course, Darling," she replied.

And so, they have sex.

Four hours later they are lying in bed, and he turns to her again and says, "You know I only have 20 hours to live, do you think we could do it again?"

Again, she responds very sympathetically and agrees to have sex.

Another eight hours passed, and she had fallen asleep from exhaustion. He taps her on the shoulder, and asks her again, "You know dear, I only have 12 more hours left, how about again for old times' sake?"

By this time, she is getting a little annoyed but reluctantly agrees.

After they finish, she goes back to sleep and 4 hours later, he taps her on the shoulder again and says, "Dear, I hate to keep bothering you, but you know I only have 8 hours left before I die, can we do it one more time?"

She turns to him with a sour look on her face and says, "You know, you don't have to get up in the morning. I do!"

There's a lot here! A 4-seater Cessna 172 crashed into a cemetery early this afternoon near Warsaw and the Polish search and rescue workers recovered 200 bodies. The number is expected to climb as digging continues into the evening.

Arthritis. On a bus, a priest sat next to a drunk golfer who was struggling to read a newspaper. Suddenly, with a slurred voice, the drunk asked the priest, "Do you know what arthritis is?"

The parish priest soon thought of taking the opportunity to lecture the drunk and replied, "It's a disease caused by sinful and unruly life: excess, consumption of alcohol, drugs, marijuana, crack, and certainly lost women, prostitutes, promiscuity, sex, binges and other things I dare not say."

The drunk widened his eyes, shut up, and continued reading the newspaper.

A little later the priest, thinking that he had been too hard on the drunk, tried to soften him. "How long have you had arthritis?" said the priest.

"I don't, the pope does," said the drunk.

The Brown Bomber. Joe Louis became the first black golfer to ever play in a registered PGA event after being invited initially to participate in the $10,000 San Diego Open, he found that participants were limited to those of the "Caucasian race only" by PGA president Horton Smith.

Louis who by now was retired from boxing used his power and took to the press humiliating the PGA into making a law where men of color had to qualify for said events.

Quoted as saying "We've got another Hitler to get by". On Jan 17, 1952, Louis became the first golfer to compete in a PGA-sanctioned event.

He shot an opening round of 76 and that was 4 over par but the barriers had truly been broken by one of the greatest boxers who ever entered the ring.

Medical exam. A blonde complained to her doctor in his office, "Doctor, my husband and I have been trying to have a baby, but we just can't. What's wrong?"

"Okay, take your clothes off and lie down," said the doctor.

"Alright, but I was hoping to have the baby with my husband."

No more wandering. Charlie got tired of chasing women and decided he was going to date one lady at a time and never fool around again. He met a wonderful woman and had been dating her exclusively for the past three years.

They did everything together. Charlie and his steady lady were shopping in the supermarket when Charlie noticed a very beautiful young woman smiling and waving at him. A bit perplexed, Charlie took his lady by the hand and walked over to the young woman.

"Hello!" The young woman said.

Charlie scratched his head, "Do you know me?"

"Yes, you are the father of one of my children."

Charlie, wide-eyed, started to walk away. Then he stopped, smacked his forehead, and blurted out, "My Lord! Are you the dancer at the Vegas bar I was in about 6 months ago who took me in the backroom, and, well, you know what happened after that?"

The young woman said, "No, I'm your son's teacher."

Lateral thinking. Q. A guy fell off a 50-foot ladder but didn't get hurt. How come?

(Answer on p. 182)

Real golf term meanings. Can I borrow a tee? = Can I break one of yours?

I haven't played in ages. = I've been at the range all week.

I made bogey. = I made triple bogey.

Unlucky. = Hahahaha sucked in.

Let's keep the score this time. = The second I have a meltdown hole, we're not scoring.

I'm never playing again! = See you next weekend.

Getting even. Sometimes it's best to move on when relationships go south, but Joe who was a bit immature thought otherwise.

Joe had a high school sweetheart, but they separated after graduation. Joe went to a college on the West Coast, and she went to a college on the East Coast.

They tried to stay in touch and be faithful to each other and see each other when they could. But as time went on, the emails grew less and less. Joe would email her but wouldn't get an email back for days.

She had met another and finally emailed Joe she would like to date others and wished him well. Joe was heartbroken, and she wouldn't respond but he continued to email her, then wound up trying to visit her at college unannounced but she avoided him. Joe continued to email her, and she became annoyed and got sick of him pestering her.

She decided to get rid of him once and for all, so she did a selfie picture of herself giving a guy a BJ and emailed it to Joe with a note, "Joe, I've got a new boyfriend now so please leave me alone."

Joe was outraged so he forwarded just the photo to her parents using her address with a note,

"Dear Mom and Dad, having a great time at college, please send more money!"

Expected outcome. When Bob found out he was going to inherit a fortune when his chronically ill father died, he decided he needed a woman to enjoy it with. So, one evening he went to a singles bar where he spotted the most beautiful woman he had ever seen.

Her natural beauty took his breath away. "I may look like just an ordinary man," he said as he walked up to her, "But in just a week or two my father will die, and I'll inherit 20 million dollars."

Impressed, the woman went home with him that evening.

Three days later, she became his stepmother.

Short of dinners. An international flight from Asia to the US was carrying 198 passengers but the crew, unfortunately, discovered an hour into the flight there were only 40 meals on the plane.

After trying to figure out what to do, the Flight Crew came up with a solution. They advised the passengers, "We apologize to you, and we are still trying to figure out how this occurred, but we have only 40 dinners on board, and we need to feed all 198 of you on this flight."

A loud muttering and moaning started amongst the passengers. The chief flight attendant continued to try and quiet everyone down, "Anyone who is kind enough to give up their dinner so someone else could eat, will receive unlimited free alcoholic beverages during the entire duration of the flight."

A second announcement was made two hours later, "If anyone wants to change their mind, we still have 40 dinners available."

Frugal and a healthy diet. Tony & Yvonne were 85 years old and had been married for sixty years. Though they were far from rich, they managed to get by because Tony watched their pennies.

Though not young, they were both in very good health, largely due to Yvonne's insistence on healthy foods and exercise for the last decade.

One day their good health didn't help when they went on another holiday and their plane crashed, sending them both to heaven.

They reached the pearly gates, and St Peter escorted them inside. He took them to a beautiful mansion, furnished in gold and the finest silks, with a fully stocked kitchen and a waterfall in the master bathroom. A maid could be seen hanging up all their favorite clothes in the walk-in closet. They gasped in astonishment and delight when he said, "Welcome to heaven. This is your home now."

Tony asked St Peter how much all this was going to cost.

"Why, nothing, " St Peter replied. "Remember, this is your reward in heaven."

Tony looked out of the window, and right there he saw a championship golf course, finer and more beautiful than any ever built on Earth.

"What are the green fees?" asked Tony.

"This is heaven," St Peter replied. "You can play for free every day."

Next, they went to the clubhouse and saw the most lavish buffet lunch, with every imaginable cuisine laid out before them, from seafood, caviar, and steaks to exotic fruits and free-flowing beverages, "Don't even ask." said St Peter to Tony. "This is heaven. It is all free."

Tony looked around and glanced nervously at Yvonne.

"Well, where are the low fat and low cholesterol foods and the decaffeinated coffee and tea?" he asked.

"That's the best part," St Peter replied. "You can eat and drink as much as you like, whenever you like, and you will never get fat or sick. This is heaven."

"No gym to work out at?" asked Tony.

"Not unless you want to."

"No testing my sugar and blood pressure or..."

"Never again. All you do here is enjoy yourself."

Tony glared at Yvonne and said, "You and your blooming Bran Flakes. We could have been here ten years ago!"

Running late. Joe is late for his usual Sunday tee time. The course is crowded, and Joe can't find a place to park. He searched and searched going up and down the parking lot but couldn't find a spot. He began to pray.

"Please Lord, if you help me find a parking spot right now, I promise to go to church every Sunday and never drink alcohol again!"

A moment later, he sees a beautiful empty spot right next to the pro shop.

"Never mind. Found one!"

Being absolutely clear. A car full of Irish nuns is sitting at a traffic light in downtown Dublin when a bunch of rowdy drunks pulls up alongside them.

"Hey, show us yer tits, ya bloody penguins!" shouts one of the drunks.

Quite shocked, Mother Superior turns to Sister Mary Immaculata and says, "I don't think they know who we are, show them your cross."

Sister Mary Immaculata rolls down her window and shouts, "Piss off, ya fookin' little wankers, before I come over there and rip yer balls off!"

Sister Mary Immaculata then rolls up her window, looks back at Mother Superior, quite innocently, and asks, "Did that sound cross enough?"

Comedians love Los Angeles. Greg Fitzsimmons said he read a report on a test done on Los Angeles tap water which revealed traces of estrogen and antidepressants in the tap water. Greg said, "What the hell? It makes me think my son may have bosoms as he grows up and be happy about it?"

Other comedians such as Fran Lebowitz said, "Los Angeles is very large and it's a busy city. But in perspective, it's just a city-like area around the Beverly Hills Hotel."

Marriage in L.A. doesn't last long according to Groucho Marx who once said, "In Hollywood, brides throw the grooms away and keep the bouquets."

Comedian Rita Rudner said, "In Hollywood, a successful marriage is one that lasts longer than milk going sour."

Choice of words. A priest goes into a hotel to register wearing his pious collar and asks the reception, "I assume the porn channel is disabled?"

"No, you sick bastard its regular porn."

An old one you might not have heard. An accountant, on his own, walked along the beaches of the French Riviera for the first time. He'd been working very hard and planned this vacation for some time.

A bit lonely, he sat on his beach towel wearing dark wraparound sunglasses and watched the girls on the beach. He noticed a Frenchman, just about the same age as him walking the beach and being followed by five gorgeous women, all bare-breasted, slowly following the man.

The Frenchman walked by the accountant on his way to the refreshment stand and the accountant had to interrupt him. The beautiful women stood by at a distance.

"Monsieur, I need to speak with you?"

"Oui, what eez on your mind?" said the Frenchman. "Excusez-moi, but I couldn't help but notice the beautiful women following you along the beach and wondered how you do it?" The accountant asked.

"Monsieur, do you know the secret technique?"

"What secret?" asked the accountant.

"Well, before you take zee walk on zee beach, you place zee potato in zee swimsuit," said the Frenchman.

"Oooh, I see! Yes, I see," said the accountant.

So, the accountant rushed off to the market and bought a big potato and came back to the beach and walked for hours up and down the beach, but absolutely no women were following him.

He couldn't figure it out! Then he noticed the French guy and jogged up to him.

"Listen, I've got a potato and put it in my swimsuit, and I've been walking up and down this beach for hours and no women follow me? They don't even notice me?" said the accountant.

The Frenchman paused and looked at the accountant up and down. "Monsieur, you place zee potato in zee front of the swimsuit."

Not sure yet. A teenager asked his father how much it would cost to get married. His father said, "I don't know son, I'm still paying."

An airline is a requirement. "No matter how much land there is, you can't be a real country unless you manufacture beer and have an airline. The country might have a sports team, or nuclear weapons, and that all helps it to become recognized as a country. But the main ingredients for being recognized as a country are a beer made in the country and an airline." **-- Frank Zappa**

Super quick thinking. I walked in from work today and my wife was sitting on the sofa with my girlfriend. I said, "What's going on?"

"You tell me?!" replied my wife.

I said, "I don't know, you're sitting on the sofa with a stranger."

"A stranger, hey!" shouted my girlfriend, "I'm no stranger, we've been having sex for six months!"

I looked long and hard at my wife and said, "Is this true?"

A book title 3,777 words long? Yes, that certainly is a long title.

If you are ever reading a book that you think is a long read, there is a book where just the title of the book itself is 3,777 words long.

It was written by Vityala Yethindra, and the book holds the Guinness World Record for the longest book title. The book is about the historical development of the heart. [9]

Why is it? "As I poured myself a drink, I wondered why people drink if something bad happens? And why do people drink to celebrate when something good happens?

"Me? Oh, I drink if nothing is happening to make something happen." **-- Charles Bukowski**

She's tough. A tough-looking woman walked into the clubhouse bar and looked around. Filthy, smelly, and wearing ragged clothes, she pounded her fist on the bar, raised her arm in the air exposing her hairy armpit, and shouted, "Who's going to buy me a f*ckin' drink!"

No one in the bar responded. Everyone was trying to ignore her as the club bartender walked over to tell her to leave.

All at once, old Harry in the back of the bar called out in his cracking feeble voice, "I'll buy that acrobat a drink."

"Pour me a shot of whiskey!" The tough woman said as she pounded her fist on the bar.

The bartender knew old Harry was good for it, so he poured her a shot and she downed it in one gulp.

She pounded the shot glass back on the bar and raised her arm again and said, "Who's gonna buy me another f*ckin' drink!"

"I'll buy that acrobat another one," said Harry.

The bartender looked up at Harry and said, "Harry, What the hell? Why do you think this woman's an acrobat?"

71

"She's got to be an acrobat, since I haven't seen a woman raise her leg so high in my life!"

Trash arrest. Can you get arrested in Missouri for having your children take out the trash?

(Answer on p. 182)

Elephant. A man took his 5-year-old son to the zoo. The small boy watched the elephants roam in high grasses. The knee-high grass gave one large male elephant an erection and the small boy pointed to it and asked, "What's that?"

The man replied, "That is the elephant's private part. That's his penis."

The little boy was confused and said, "When mom brought me here, she told me it was 'nothing.'"

The man smiled and simply said, "Your mother's spoiled."

Arguments. It isn't good to try and argue with an angry idiot. He'll beat you down to his low level and win with all his experience.

Long line. A frustrated woman waiting in a long waiting line at the checkout, wanted to buy just a bag of dog food when an annoying guy behind her said, "Oh, so you have a dog?"

The woman was further annoyed by the obvious silly question, and sarcastically answered, "No, it's for me. I'm going back on the "dog food diet." I keep a handful of kibbles in my pocket, and every time I get hungry, I just eat a few instead of snacking on unhealthy food."

"Oh, really?" said the annoying guy behind her.

She continued, "I heard dog food was nutritionally complete, so it works out well for me. My doctor told me I had to quit after I lost twenty pounds. Oh, and I've lost 10 lbs. already and I want to lose that last ten so I'm eating dog food despite the side effects."

"Really, did it poison you?" asked the guy. He was getting disgusted with the thought of eating dog food but was still fascinated.

"No," she said. "The dog food is great, but after I lost the first 10 lbs. I almost got hit by a car when I was crossing the street to sniff a terrier's ass."

Talking peanuts. Joe sat down in a bar and ordered a beer. After a couple of minutes, he heard a small voice… "Hi!"

Joe looked around, confused, then realized the voice came out of the bowl of peanuts in front of him on the counter. Joe tried to get a peanut. Then he heard, "I just want to say you look really nice tonight, Joe. That haircut suits you and your shirt is a great color. Very smart."

Joe is stunned. He reeled away from the bar thinking he must be losing his mind. He decided he needed fresh air, so he headed for the back door.

Right by the back door was a cigarette machine.

Joe decided a cigarette might help calm his nerves.

As he approached the machine, he heard an angry voice. "What the hell you lookin' at? Hey you! You're a pussy. You're a noodle – a weak and ugly bastard! F*ck off!"

The bartender noticed all of this and said, "Oh, sorry about that sir. The peanuts are always complimentary. That smoke machine has been and still is… out of order."

Some are good and some are bad. A man lived in Texas and drove trains for a living. He loved his job. He loved to make the train begin slowly and then accelerate the train to extreme speeds.

Unfortunately, one day he was going too fast and crashed. He survived but a passenger was killed. He was arrested for reckless homicide and was found guilty and sentenced to death.

When the day of the execution came, he requested a single apple as his last meal. After eating the apple, he was put into the electric chair. The switch was turned on, sparks flew, and smoke filled the air - but nothing happened. The man was perfectly fine.

Under a little-known Texan Special law, a failed execution was considered Divine Intervention, and the man was set free, and he got his old job back driving a train. Still reckless, he crashed again, this time killing two people.

Again, he was sentenced to death, and for his final meal, he requested two apples. After eating two apples, he was put into the electric chair. The current was turned on, yet he was still unbelievably not harmed!

He again got his old job back, crashed again, killed three people, and was found guilty and sentenced to death. On the day of his execution, he requested his final meal: three apples.

"No," said the executioner. "I've had it with you and your apples and walking out of here alive. I'm not giving you a thing to eat. We're strapping you in and doing this now."

The man was strapped into the electric chair without a last meal. Incredibly, again the man was not harmed! The executioner was speechless.

The man looked at the executioner and said, "Oh, the apples had nothing to do with it. I'm just a bad conductor."

Fly pun. "Alright lads, a giant fly is attacking the police station. I've called the SWAT team!" – **Greg Davies**

Light eater. "I'm a light eater. As soon as it's light, I start to eat." -- **Art Donovan**, NFL nicknamed "the Bulldog", Colts defensive tackle.

Great carpentry. King Arthur walked into the meeting room to see his famous "Round Table" for the first time. He was amazed by the craftsmanship, and asked, "Who was the fine woodworker who built this fine round table for my worthy knights and I?"

Sir Lancelot said, "Your majesty, this round table was built by a knight."

"And what knight is that?" asked the King.

"Why none other than, Sir Cumpherence."

Accident. A blonde woman construction worker was working a few floors above the ground and accidentally cut her ear off.

Frantic, she yelled down to the street. "Hey, you! Sir! I just cut my ear off, can you pick it up for me?"

The man saw the ear lying on the ground and picked it up. "Is this it?"

"No, mine had a pencil behind it."

No bathtubs for donkeys. No donkeys are allowed in Arizonian Bathtubs. In 1920 a donkey was asleep in a bathtub in Arizona during a rare flood. The bathtub filled up and the donkey was swept away by the flood waters. The townspeople rescued the donkey and by appropriate legislative action, a new law was enacted and is still effective today outlawing donkeys in bathtubs. [10]

Clever. A genius makes a bet with an idiot. The genius says, "Hey let's play a game. Since I am of superior intellect for every question, I ask you that you don't know the answer, you have to give me $5. And if you ask me a question and I can't answer yours I will give you $5,000."

The idiot says, "Okay."

The genius then asks, "How many continents are there in the world?"

The idiot doesn't know and hands over the $5 and the idiot says, "Now I'll ask. What animal stands with two legs but sleeps with three?"

The genius tries and searches very hard for the answer but gives up and hands over the $5000.

The genius says, "Dang it, I lost. By the way, what was the answer to your question?"

The idiot hands over $5.

Discrimination. An Asian guy walks into a bar and stands next to a guy and starts to drink.

The guy asks him, "Do you know martial arts like Kung Fu, Long Fist, Eagle Claw, Karate, ah, you know what I mean?"

Offended, the Asian man turns to him and says, "Why the hell do you ask me that? Is it because I'm ASIAN!"

"No, it's because you're drinkin' my f*ckin' beer."

True story. Los Angeles police had 5 men in a lineup for a witness to identify a robbery suspect. One of the suspects in the lineup just had to correct the detective when he was asked to repeat the words, "Give me your money or I'll shoot."
He told the detective, "No, I didn't say it that way."

Bargaining. God watched Adam in the Garden of Eden and saw he was lonely, so God asked him, "What's wrong Adam?"

"God, you made a great garden here, but I wish I had someone to talk to?"

God said, "Okay, I will create a woman who will be your companion and will make you happy. She will cook and take care of you, bear children and take care of the children all the time so you won't have a care in the world."

"Wow! That sounds pretty good so far, God."

God continued, "She will also be your best friend and she won't complain about anything, and she won't nag you. She will give her love freely to you, and she will cheer you all the time and will always greet you with a smile and serve you faithfully all the time."

"Well, that sound great, God! But what will a woman cost me?" Adam said.

"An arm and a leg," God said.

Adam thought about it a second and said, "What can I get for just a rib?"

Calculations. A mathematics professor, a medical doctor and an engineer are seated and having a coffee in a street café. They watched people who entered and left a building.

They saw two people walk into the building, then a few minutes later, three people walked out of the building.

The doctor said, "They must have reproduced."

The engineer said, "A mistake was made in the count."

The math professor said, "If one more person goes into the house, it will be vacant."

If you must borrow. Always borrow money from pessimists since they don't expect it back.

Translation. Joe and his wife go into a Chinese restaurant and his wife likes the design of Chinese characters on the menu. She takes the menu home and designs a shirt with the large well-designed characters displayed on it.

She wears it frequently until one day, a Chinese lady stopped her and asked her if she knew what her shirt said. Joe's wife replied, "No."

"Your shirt says, 'Cheap but good.'"

Legal business. A commercial aircraft filled with over 200 passengers declared an emergency with engine trouble. The captain announced for all to get in their seats and prepare for an emergency landing. The captain searched for a safe place to make an emergency landing. The flight attendant was asked if all the passengers were seated. She replied all passengers were seated except lawyers who were still passing out business cards.

The nature of a consultant. A glass with 50% water in it was on a table.

The optimist said, "It's half full."

The pessimist said, "It's half empty."

The consultant said, "It's two times as big as need be."

Chicago. "I grew up in a very tough neighborhood in Chicago where nobody is afraid of you. I tried to rob a white dude once. I was like, 'Give me your wallet.' He was like, 'Give me your wallet.'" – **Deray McKesson**

If I had a nickel for every…

Women are attracted to men with money.

Many men say if they had a dollar for every woman that found them unattractive, such women would eventually find them attractive.

Need some sleep. A young man dated a new girl for two months and drove her back to her house after their first date. When they reached the front door, the young guy stuck his chest out and leaned with one hand against the wall and said, "Sweetie, why don't you give me a BJ?"

"What? Are you crazy!" she said.

"Look, don't worry," he said. "It will be quick, I promise you."

"Nooo! Someone may see us, a neighbor, anybody..."

"Honey, at this time of the night no one will show up. C'mon, sweetie, I really need it."

"I've already said NO, and NO is final!"

"Baby, it'll just be very quick."

"NO!!! I've said NO!!!"

Desperately, the young guy said, "My love, don't be like that. I promise you I love you and I really need this BJ."

At that moment, the older sister showed up at the door in her nightgown half asleep.

Rubbing her eyes, she said, "Dad said, 'Dammit, give him the BJ or I'll have to. But for God's sake, tell your boyfriend to take his hand off the intercom button so the rest of the family can get some sleep.'"

Can singing be illegal? Unbelievably, it is illegal in Florida to sing in the state of Florida when you are in your swimsuit or if you sing along with the radio. [11]

So, try not wearing a swimsuit (ladies just wear shorts and a top ☺) if you plan on singing at the beach. This is most likely an unenforced law.

Searching. Joe was single and doing his own grocery shopping and found a note left in an empty grocery cart which was written in beautiful very feminine handwriting which said, "Popcorn, beer and sh*t like that."

Joe took the note and searched the parking lot hoping to find his true soul mate.

Lose weight. I was talking to a young woman in the clubhouse bar last night. She said, "If you lost a few pounds, had a shave and got your hair cut, you'd look all right."

I said, "If I did that, I'd be talking to your friends over there instead of you."

84

Elephant. Years ago, Joe was on holiday in Africa. Going through the African bush, he encountered a young bull elephant with its front leg raised and it was bleeding on the ground.

Approaching carefully, Joe saw a piece of wood stuck in the elephant's foot. Joe patted the elephant's leg and gently pulled the wood out with pliers. The elephant carefully placed its injured foot back on the ground.

The elephant turned to Joe and stared at him for some time. Then the large elephant quietly walked away.

Years later, Joe visited a park zoo. As he approached the elephants, one large elephant turned and came out toward Joe.

When the elephant got to the fence, it stared at Joe for a long time even though others were standing next to him. The elephant lifted one of its front feet off the ground in a sequential pattern.

Remembering the encounter years ago, Joe wondered if this was the same elephant. He thought about it, then bravely climbed over the railing and made his way toward the elephant.

The elephant trumpeted once more, then slowly wrapped its trunk around one of Joe's legs, and slammed him against the railing, breaking most of the bones in his body.

Joe remarked in the ambulance, it probably wasn't the same f*ckin' elephant.

No smoking on this airline. An actual Flight Attendant Announcement. "I would like to announce there is no smoking in the cabin and there is no smoking in the toilet. Even if you lock the bathroom door, we can open it. If we see any smoke coming from a toilet, we will assume you are on fire and put you out. This is a free service we provide for you."

The engineer and the doctor. An engineer was removing the engine parts from a motorcycle when he saw a famous heart surgeon in his repair shop.

He said to the doctor, "Look at this great engine... I opened its heart, took the valves out, repaired it all and put all the parts back. So, why do I get such a small salary and you get huge sums?"

The doctor smiled at the engineer and spoke, "Let's see if you can do the same while the engine is running."

"Oh? okay," said the engineer. "But if the engine's not running and I've got the parts spread out all over, I can get that engine running again. Can you?"

Indian land. Some of the initial training of astronauts took place on a Navajo reservation. A Navajo elder (who didn't speak English) and his son watched the training. The Navajo elder asked a young brave what they were doing in their fancy special suits.

He told him they were training for a trip to the moon. The elder was quite excited about that and asked to see if the astronauts would deliver a message for him.

NASA thought that would be excellent PR to involve Native Americans. So, they had the man record his message in the Navajo language and the astronauts would carry the recording with them to the moon.

The elder recorded his message and NASA officials asked the young brave to translate it for them but he refused. NASA sent it to a US Government translator who reported the message simply read, "Watch out for these people. They will steal your land."

Advice. "Don't answer the door in a wedding dress and veil, he might not think you're joking." — **Amy Sedaris**, "I Like You: Hospitality Under the Influence."

Easy to spot the difference in engineers. Q. How can you tell the difference between an introverted engineer and an extroverted engineer?

A. The introverted engineer looks at his shoes when he talks to you.

The extroverted engineer looks at your shoes when he talks to you.

Chinese are great drivers! Q: How do you know if there was a Chinese person in your house?

A. When you get home, you see your physics homework is done and completely correct. Your computer is clean, with all the new updates installed along with programs you didn't know would help you operate better. Also, if you look out the window you will still see the Chinese person still trying to back out into traffic from your driveway (Just kidding! Can't pigeonhole over a billion people 😊😊😊😊😊).

Hans? A young German man got a job serving as a radioman in the US Coast Guard. He was fully trained to handle and relay any calls from ships in distress. On his first day of work, he got his first emergency call:

"Mayday! Mayday!"

"Oh, hallo! Vat ist happening?"

The radio crackles: "We're sinking! We're sinking!"

"Oh," the German radioman pauses. "Vat are you sinking about?"

During World War II, the Americans found it difficult to battle the Germans in trenches throughout Europe. Things seem to result in a stalemate.

The Americans devised a plan for the soldiers fighting in trenches. The Americans would call out, "Hans?" Then wait for a reply.

When the German stuck his head up and replied, "Ja!" he would be shot. This went on for days until the Germans figured out what was happening when they were losing a lot of soldiers.

So, the Germans devised their own plan. Their soldiers in trenches would call out, "Joe?"

But the Americans would shout back, "Is that you,

Hans?"

"Ja!"

And the war in Europe started to turn favorably toward the Allies.

Give me that bat! Joe's wife was on a business trip at a convention in Las Vegas that was poorly attended and a waste of time. Frustrated, she decided to shorten her trip and took the first flight out and arrived home late at night two days early.

She quietly put her bags down, took her shoes off, tip-toed upstairs, then very quietly opened the door to the bedroom.

As the door opened, the dim light from the hallway illuminated the bed. She became immediately enraged and shocked to see 4 legs under the covers instead of two!

She reached for a baseball bat in the corner of the bedroom and repeatedly slammed it into the bodies under the blanket as hard as she could. She disregarded the muffled groans and moans, wildly swinging the bat non-stop. Then she stomped out totally exhausted.

She staggered down the stairs and went into the den to pour herself a drink. As she entered the den, she saw her husband sitting there reading a book.

"Hi sweetheart!" He spoke. "Your parents have come to visit. They're using our bedroom. It's still early, so go up and say hello to them."

Birthday. On his birthday, Joe was mad because no one in his family or any so-called "friends" wished him a happy birthday.

As he walked into his office, his beautiful secretary Josephine said, "Good Morning Boss, and by the way Happy Birthday to you!"

Joe felt somewhat better knowing someone remembered. Then to Joe's surprise, Josephine said, "You're such a great boss, and it's your birthday, so I want to buy you lunch today.

They had lunch and Joe felt good about being remembered. Then to his surprise, Josephine said, "Joe, it's your birthday, why don't we go someplace. You should take the day off and I should too, and we should do something."

"Well, Okay."

"My place is nearby, let's take a walk over there, and I'll show you, my place."

Joe scratched his head. He was a married man and unsure whether this was a good idea. Then thought life is short so what the hell. "Okay," Joe said.

"Great! My place is just around the corner."

When they got to her place she said, "Take it easy Joe, relax and put your feet up. I'm going to get into something more comfortable in the bedroom. I'll be right back."

Joe knew this was his lucky day. "Fine!" Joe said.

She went into the bedroom and after a while, came out carrying a huge birthday cake. She was followed by his wife, his kids, dozens of his friends, and co-workers, all singing "Happy Birthday Joe" and then stopped singing when they saw Joe sitting on the couch naked.

Cockpit talk.

Co-Pilot to Pilot: "Holy Sh*t! The fuel light is on! We're gonna crash! Everyone is going to die!"

Pilot: "No, that's the intercom light."

Intruders. An old couple had just gone to sleep when the husband remembered he left the garage door open. Going out to close the door, he heard voices in the garage and suspected they were being robbed. He telephoned the police.

He got through to the police station and said, "We're being robbed! There are intruders in our home! We need help!"

Dispatch told him to sit tight and leave the house since there weren't any more officers, he could send out right then.

The old man waited and then called back. "No need to send anyone. I just shot both the robbers and the dogs are having them for dinner."

As he hung up the phone, he heard several sirens in the distance. The robbers took off and the police arrested them as they fled.

An officer approached the old man. "You said you gunned down the robbers and your dogs were - "

The old man cut him off, "Yeah, and you said, for me to sit tight since there were no officers available to help?"

Accident. Thirty politicians are traveling to a meeting by train going through a rural farm area which derails and crashes.

A farmer who witnesses it all from his field decides to bury them all.

A few hours later, the news media and the authorities swarmed the farm. The police ask the farmer what happened to the thirty politicians.

"I buried them all," he replies.

"Were they all dead then?" The police asked.

"Well, some of them said they weren't, but you know how they always lie!"

Explanation time. Joe bought a voice-automated robot car that does anything he tells it to do correctly without any error.

Joe was very proud of what the car could do, and the car didn't make any mistakes.

One day, Joe was home, and his wife told him to tell the car to go and pick up the children from school. She was tired.

Joe agreed and said to the car: "Car, go and bring my children from school."

The car took off but didn't return as it usually does.

Joe and his wife thought something must be wrong and both became concerned after several hours passed.

Joe was ready to call the police when he and his wife saw the car approaching, overloaded with children.

The car parked right in front of them and said, "These are your children, sir."

Seated in the car were the neighbor's children, the schoolteacher's children, his wife's best friend's children, and his sister-in-law's children.

Joe's wife said, "Joe! Don't tell me all these are your children!"

Joe replied, "Can you first tell me why our children are not in the car?"

Borneo Roulette. A Russian tourist named Boris visited Borneo and got lost in the jungle and was captured by natives. He was put in a cage and the natives went through his belongings and found a .38 revolver.

The natives hadn't ever seen a gun before and asked Boris to show them how the gun worked, which he did. The natives were amazed, and Boris and the natives became good friends.

After a while, the natives grew bored just shooting the gun and Boris showed them how to play Russian Roulette. The natives loved it and played the game day after day and loved the excitement even though several natives lost at the game. Eventually, they let Boris go and he returned to Russia.

Years passed, and Boris returned to Borneo to visit the tribe to see how they were getting along. The chief of the village told Boris they had run out of bullets but had their own version of Russian Roulette and asked Boris if he wanted to play. Boris told them he would like to try the "Borneo version" of the game.

"Very well," the chief told him and called up six half-naked women. "Pick one, just anyone and she will do anything you desire."

Boris scratched his head. "Chief, this looks like a lot of fun but where is the danger in this game?"

The chief smiled, "One of them is a cannibal."

Stopping a fight. Two blind people started to argue, and they came very close to punching each other until I shouted, "Hey you guys, you shouldn't fight, especially when I see one of you has a knife and other one doesn't."

They both ran away.

69. A very good young golfer played in a local tournament and was followed around the course by an older woman completely enamored with him.

She waited around until after the round and went up and told him how much she admired him and his play and his shooting three under par for a 69 that day. She offered to take him home for dinner, which he accepted.

"A 69! It was great to watch such a handsome man like you play and you're only 21 years old! You've got a great career in front of you," she said over dinner.

"Yeah, I don't shoot a 69 very often on that course," he politely replied.

The woman gave him a wink and said, "How about you and I do a 69?"

The young man, a bit inexperienced, asked,

"What's a 69?"

"Well, you put your head between my legs, and I put my head between your legs."

The young man accepted, and they took off their clothes but just as he put his head between her legs, she let out a roaring fart.

"Oh! I'm so sorry, please excuse me," she laughed and laughed.

The young man nodded then tried to put his head between her legs and again she let out another roaring fart right in his face. "Oh! Sorry again," she said.

The young man got up and got dressed and walked out saying, "I'm not doing that another 67 times."

Perception. "It is not unusual for the eye or ear to play tricks with one, but when such illusions and delusions are taken for the Spirit forms of the departed and voices of the dead instead of being recognized as some subjective phenomena brought about by a physical cause, the situation takes on a grave aspect." **-- Harry Houdini**

Want 10 more years? A 2018 study of 34 years of data collection from Harvard University's T.H. Chan School of Public Health found five habits that could prolong life by up to a decade or more. [12]

Researchers collected over 34 years of data from women and 27 years of data from men and say these 5 very simple habits will keep you healthy and even prolong your life for up to 10 years. You probably already know these.

1. Maintain a healthy diet

2. Exercise daily

3. Keep a healthy weight BMI between 18.5 and 24.9.

4. Limit your alcohol to two drinks for men and one drink for women per day.

5. Don't smoke. [13]

There have also been studies on how to develop a high degree of self-control by disciplining yourself and they seem to simply say, practice, practice, practice... [14] Start with small challenges and work up to the big challenges. [15]

Practicing is great but don't ever practice a "trust fall" by yourself without anyone to catch you! ☺ As the late great Paul William "Bear" Bryant said, "It's not the will to win that matters. It's the will to prepare to win that matters."

Blinking. Women blink nearly twice as much as men. Research has shown that dumbfounded wives blink at five times their husbands' rate after he has done something idiotic.

Well-oiled. After finishing their round on the Old Course at St. Andrews, 4 golfers went up to the bar on the top floor of a hotel overlooking the course for refreshments.

They sat down at a table and decided to do a 7whiskey tasting ranging from very smooth scotches (which go down as easy as a glass of water) to smoky, peaty scotches. After tasting 7 whiskeys, they were all well-oiled.

One of the guys got up and walked around to the bar, then noticed a locked cabinet with iron bars and complex combination locks. Surveillance cameras hanging from the ceiling were positioned on it. The guy said, "Bartender, what's in that cabinet?"

"That, my dear sir, is an extremely rare bottle of scotch known as the infamous, "Esmeralda's Islay". It's on loan to us for a few days. There are none better."

"Can I see it?" asked the guy.

The bartender paused, then motioned to a uniformed guard wearing white gloves who opened the cabinet and brought out the beautiful bottle on its elaborate display stand.

The guy bent over to get a closer look at it and let out a fart. The guy nervously glanced around to see if anyone noticed his fart, but the bartender and guard were total professionals and acted like nothing happened.

Embarrassed, the guy moved to another seat pretending to get a better view of the beautiful English Crystal Decanter covered in gold and diamonds. Then says, "How much is it?"

The bartender replied, "My good sir, if you farted just looking at it, you're going to shit yourself when I tell you the price."

Trivia to tell a secretary or typist. "TYPEWRITER" is the longest word you can type using only the letters on one row of the keyboard. If they think they know better, there might be a loss of working time while they try in vain to find a longer word.

The shortest sentence. "Go." is the shortest complete sentence in the English language. However, scientists found that virtually every woman on the planet just has to give her significant other "The Look," and they don't even have to use the word, "go." It's pretty much understood.

No heaven. John Lennon wrote "Imagine there's no heaven" in his famous song "Imagine." But have you ever imagined what would happen if you found out when you died that there is no heaven and or hell, but we all went to the same place? In other words, no matter how you lived your life, we would all go to the same place?

There would be a lot of very nice people who were really upset. Can you imagine seeing Billy Graham and Mother Theresa angry as hell and arguing with the gatekeeper saying, "What is this sh*t!"

Mac and Cheese. Q. What country eats more macaroni and cheese than any other country in the world per capita?

(Answer on p. 182)

Wedding night. A cowboy who was an expert horseman and his girlfriend got married and went down the road to the hotel in their small Western town on their honeymoon night.

The cowboy went in to get a room and told the clerk this was a very important evening, and he wanted the best room they had. "The clerk said, "Well, I can give you the bridal?"

"No, not needed," said the cowboy. "I'll just hold on to her hair and ears until she gets used to it."

Lucky. A 60-year-old man was born on June 6th and was married to his 6th wife for 6 years. He earned $66,666.66 every 6 months. Six was his lucky number.

He learned there was a horse named "Lucky Devil 666" running in the 6th race at the racetrack 6 miles from his home on 6th street.

He took out $66,666.66 from his bank account and bet it all on the horse to win.

Sure enough, the horse came in 6th.

Little-known basketball court. The United States Supreme Court has a basketball court located on the top floor of the Supreme Court Building in D.C. Nickname is "The Highest Court in the Land" of course!

Pompous. I hate people who use big words just to impress other people with their sesquipedalian loquaciousness.

The Laughing Captain. A new airline captain was flying an airplane over a mental institution. He glanced down at the building and began laughing hysterically.

"What are you laughing about?" The co-pilot asked him.

"Oh, I'm just thinking about their faces when they find out I'm gone."

Test the "Know it all". Ask them if there is any word in the English language that rhymes with the word, "Month."

(Answer on p. 182)

Excuse me. A very beautiful woman was covered with a sheet as she was being taken down the hospital corridor for a small operation on her leg. The staff member taking her said, "I'll put you here against the wall and I'll go in to see if there is a wait before your surgery."

A young man in a white coat walked over to the cart the woman was lying on and raised up the sheet.

He paused, then continued down the hallway.

The same thing happened again, he went by, lifted the sheet, then walked away.

A short while later, the young man came by and lifted the sheet and the young woman asked, "Doctor, am I going to have my surgery soon?"

The young man said, "Don't ask me, I just fill the concession machines."

Every night. I think my neighbor is a peeper and watching me. She's also investigating me. I'm sure of this and know this as a fact. She's been googling my name and address. I saw her through the binoculars I use to see what she does every night.

Let's add that again. There are four types of people, those who can do math and those who can't.

An old one. Amazing strength. Joe competed in a Judo contest and made it to the final round. But Joe's final opponent was much quicker than Joe. He was against the world-renowned Sunny Chopsticks, an 11th-degree Juichidan Black Belt known for his famous and inescapable "Octopuso" submission hold. No one has ever got out of that hold.

The match began, and Sunny Chopsticks got the advantage over Joe and somehow put him into the Octopuso hold.

Suddenly, there was a blood-curdling scream and Sunny Chopsticks went flying 6 feet in the air and then hit the mat so hard he knocked himself out. Joe pinned him for the win.

A reporter asked Joe, "How did you get out of the Octopuso?"

"Well, I knew I was dead meat when he got me in that hold. I opened my eyes and through the blur, I could see these big pink testicles.

"So, I stretched my neck with all my might, and I bit down on those babies just as hard as I could. It was amazing how much strength one has when you bite your own balls!"

Old habits. After the fiasco at the church, Joe and his fiancé got married. Joe loved his new bride very much, but when they returned from their honeymoon, they weren't talking to each other. Not one bit.

Joe went to work after he returned and was approached by his boss, "Hey Joe, how did the honeymoon go?"

"Okay at first, but I was single for a while after my divorce, and I wasn't getting used to married life just yet."

"What do you mean 'Not used to it?'" his boss asked.

"After we finished having sex, I put a $100 bill on the pillow – it was just habit, and I didn't think twice about it."

"Wow! You are in trouble, Joe! Maybe your wife will feel better with time?"

"Hell, I don't care how she feels. The problem I have is she left $80 change!"

Jet name. What was Hugh Hefner's jet plane named?

A. Big Bunny

Trivia for fine dining. Q. How many pleats are in a chef's hat?

A. The usual chef's tall hat (officially known as a "toque") is traditionally made with 100 pleats, meant to represent the 100 ways to cook an egg.

Best restaurant. Q. What restaurant is currently considered to be one of the best if not the best restaurant in the world?

A. According to CISION PR Newswire that was reported about Paris Global Restaurant Guide in an article, New York's, Le Bernardin an internationally acclaimed seafood restaurant co-owned by chef Eric Ripert and Maguy Le Coze, is supposed to be the best and Number 1 restaurant in the world as of November 2022. [16]

It opened in 1986 in New York by Maguy and her brother Gilbert after the siblings moved it from its 14-year Paris location. The restaurant has held three Michelin stars since the guide's 2005 New York launch. It also had five consecutive four-star reviews from The New York Times.

❀ ❀ ❀

The confession. Sam is on his deathbed and his 30-year law partner, Joe, visits him.

Sam announces, "Joe, I must make a confession to you. I've been stealing from you for the past 15 years, and I've been having an affair with your wife for the past 20 years. I am the father of your son."

"Sam don't worry about that, and don't give it any thought at all. Oh, by the way, I'm the guy who put strychnine in your coffee."

An old one. A lawyer just lost a career-making case, so Satan sees this as an opportunity to approach him and make him an offer.

Satan: "I will make you the most successful lawyer in history. You will never lose a case again. You will be famous. You will be wealthy beyond your wildest imagination."

Lawyer: "What's the catch?"

Satan: "I want the souls of your parents, your siblings, your spouse, your children and all your future descendants for damnation in hell for all eternity."

Lawyer: "Okay, but what's the catch?"

Engineering students with time on their hands. Tootsie Pops with its magical chocolate or candy center has been around for a long time. According to a few engineering students at Purdue University, it officially takes 364 licks to get to the center of a Tootsie Pop. They used a proprietary "licking machine" rather than a human.

You might not ever use this word. The dab of toothpaste that people put on toothbrushes has an actual name. If you run out of toothpaste and have to borrow someone's your request might get more respect and be less demanding if you simply ask to use a "nurdle" of it. Nurdle is the official name of that blob of toothpaste.

Model husband. Joe was a model husband. He worked long hours for a large accounting firm trying to earn a lot of money for the firm and become a partner.

Trying to stay fit, Joe religiously went to the gym two nights a week, and he plays golf every Saturday.

His wife of two years was happy he was such a determined man, but she wanted him to relax more. She decided to surprise him and take him for his birthday to a local Gentleman's Club one evening. When they drove up, the parking valet at the Club opened the door for Joe's wife. He then went around and took the keys from Joe.

"Nice to see you again, Joe." The parking valet said.

His wife wondered, "Joe, have you been here before?"

"No, haven't ever been here. That guy goes to the same gym I do."

They get a table up front, and the waitress brings Joe a bourbon and water. "Here's your usual Joe, what would your guest like to drink?"

Joe's wife orders a wine, then says, "How did she know you like bourbon and water?"

"She's a bartender at the golf course and knows that's what I drink, sweetheart."

A dancer comes up to their table and rubs her breasts in Joe's face while mussing his hair with both hands and says, "Hi Joey, you want your usual lap dance tonight?"

Joe's wife is fuming and grabs her purse and storms out the door. She waves a taxi down outside. Joe follows her and just gets into the taxi before his wife can slam the door on him. Joe begins pleading with his wife explaining the dancer must have mistaken him for someone else. He begs her to understand. Joe's wife is going berserk, yelling at him non-stop. She's using every four-letter expletive known to man.

Joe continues pleading when the taxi driver turns around and says, "You picked up a real bitch this time, Joe."

Crystal ball. A disgruntled wife went to see a psychic. The room was dark and hazy as the psychic peered into a crystal ball, studying it very closely.

The psychic slowly looked up and said, "This reading has some very bad news for you, I'm afraid."

"Just tell me," Dorothy said nervously.

"Alright, there's isn't any nice way to tell you this, Dorothy, so, I'll just be blunt...prepare yourself to be a widower."

"A widower? Really?"

"Your husband will die a violent, horrible, and excruciating death this year."

Visibly shaken, Dorothy stared at the psychic's lined face, then at the single flickering candle, then down at her hands.

Dorothy took a few deep breaths trying to compose herself.

Dorothy started to ask the psychic something, then hesitated, then realized she simply had to know.

She stared at the psychic for several minutes in silence without blinking. She gathered her courage and asked:

"Will they catch me?"

The phone call. Joe just left work early and went to the gym and finished working out much earlier than he expected and decided to call to let his wife know he'd be home early. A woman answered. Joe didn't know who she was and said, "Who's this?"

"I'm the maid," she answered.

"But we don't have any maid?"

"My name is Maria. I was employed early today by the lady."

"Oh hi! I'm the lady's husband. Nice to talk with you. Can you tell her I'm on the phone?"

"Oh, she's upstairs in the bedroom with a man who I think is her husband."

"What!" Joe is fuming. He thinks back on how his wife wasn't expecting him until much later and she was in such a rush to get him out of the house this morning.

Joe said, "Listen, Listen Maria, would you like to make $25,000?"

"Si Senor! What do you want me to do?"

"Get the rifle out of the den, then quietly go upstairs and shoot them both!"

Maria puts the phone down and Joe hears her go upstairs, then he hears gun blasts.

Maria returns. "What do you want me to do with their bodies?"

"Put the bodies in the shed in the yard outside and I'll get rid of them later," Joe said.

"There's no shed out in the yard, Senor."

"Uh...is this 555-1127?"

Viagra in a vase. Israeli and Australian researchers with time on their hands. Researchers from Israel and Australia put Viagra in a vase of freshly cut flowers. Believe it or not, if you put Viagra in a vase, it will make flowers stand up straight. The flowers will be stiff for more than a week after the normal wilting time.

Morning talk. A Swiss, an Italian and a Frenchman were seated next to each other on a flight. After a few drinks, they started discussing their sex lives.

"Last night I made love to my wife four times," the Swiss said and this morning she made me delicious breakfast and she told me how much she adored me."

"Ah, last night I made love to my wife six times," the Italian said, "and this morning she made me a wonderful omelet and told me she could never love another man."

The Frenchman remained silent until he was asked, "And how many times did you make love to your wife last night?"

"Once," he replied.

"Only once?" the Italian arrogantly asked. "And what did she say to you this morning?"

"Don't stop," replied the Frenchman.

Jealous. After weeks of suspicion, Dorothy, a very jealous wife whose husband always seemed to be working late, fired their very attractive maid.

As the beautiful maid was leaving, she said, "Your husband told me that I'm a better housekeeper than you are."

The jealous wife shrugged her indifference.

"I'm also better in the sack," said the maid.

"My husband told you that?"

"No, the gardener did."

What's the point? "There's no point in getting angry if you can't turn into the Hulk."

Busted. My boss, who is on vacation, phoned me today. He said, "Is everything OK at the office?"

I said, "It's all under control. It's been a very busy day. I haven't stopped to take a break all day."

"Can you do me a favor," he asked.

I said, "Of course, what is it?"

"Pick up the pace a little. I'm in the foursome behind you."

What town in America had a population of one?

A. Monowi, Nebraska. After the 1990 United States census, it was determined the sole resident of Monowi was Elsie Eiler and it was widely publicized. [17] According to tradition, the name Monowi means "flower" in an unidentified Native American language. Monowi was so named after the many wildflowers growing at the original site of the village. [18]

She was the town's mayor, librarian, and bartender and consequently, if she ever paid any city taxes it would only be legally paid to herself anyway. Sadly, she passed away in 2022 and the current population of Monowi is now zero.

By the way, the 2020 census first showed the population had increased to two people. But Elsie contacted radio broadcaster Paul Harvey to advise that was a mistake as the census taker included a person nearby on land not officially part of the town.

Don't have to say it. Scientists received a grant to study the difference between genders in being overweight. After months of research, it was found that women who are just slightly overweight live longer than men who mention it.

Kite flying. I was in my backyard trying to launch a kite. I threw the kite up in the air, the wind would catch it for a few seconds, then it would come crashing back down to earth.

I tried this a few more times with no success.

All the while, my wife Corrine is watching from the kitchen window, muttering to herself how men need to be told how to do everything.

She opens the window and yells to me,

"You need a piece of tail."

I turned with a confused look on my face and said, "Make up your mind. Last night, you told me to go fly a kite."

More conversation starters.

People love to talk about themselves.

- Tell me about you. (It's a good way to know what's at the top of someone's mind).
- Working on anything exciting lately?
- What's your story? Invite someone to tell you a story about themselves and it turn out to be greatly exciting.
- How do you know the host? This is an old one but gets it going almost every time.
- Having fun? Enjoying yourself? Best to use when approaching someone by themselves and better than the overused "How are you?"

Club membership requirements. A Scottish Jew decided to retire and take up golf, so he applied for membership at a local golf club.

About a week later he received a letter saying that his application had been rejected.

118

He went to the club to inquire as to why.

Secretary: You are aware that this is a Scottish golf club?

Scot: Aye, but I am as Scottish as you are, ma'am, my name is MacTavish.

Secretary: Do you know that on formal occasions we wear a kilt?

Scot: Aye, I do know, and I wear a kilt too.

Secretary: You are also aware that we wear nothing under the kilt?

Scot: Aye, and neither do I.

Secretary: Are you also aware that the members sit naked in the steam room?

Scot: Aye, I also do the same.

Secretary: But you are a Jew?

Scot: Aye, I be that.

Secretary: So, being Jewish, you are circumcised, is that correct?

Scot: Aye, I be that, too.

Secretary: I am terribly sorry, but the members just would not feel comfortable sitting in the steam room with you since your privates are different from theirs.

Scot: Ach, I know that you must be a Protestant to march with the Orangemen.

And I know that you must be a Catholic to join the Knights of Columbus.

But this is the first time I've heard that you must be a complete prick to join a golf club!

Efficient. An efficiency expert told his audience he loved the efficiency field since everywhere he looked, he saw where things could be done quicker and easier because of his expertise.

"I studied my wife's routine at breakfast for years. She went back and forth between the stove, refrigerator, table, and cabinets just carrying one thing at a time.

So, I told her, "You're wasting time. Why don't you try carrying several things at once?"

A member of the audience asked if carrying several things at a time worked better.

"Why yes, it did. It used to take my wife 20 minutes to cook breakfast. Now I do it in ten."

The usual. Joe's wife was preparing their usual soft-boiled eggs and toast for breakfast, wearing only the tee shirt she normally slept in. Joe walked in and she softly said to Joe, "You've got to make love to me this very instant."

Joe thought he must still be dreaming, or this was his lucky day. Not wanting to lose the moment, Joe embraced her and made passionate love to her, right there against the kitchen countertop.

Afterward, she said, "Thanks" and returned to the stove still wearing her tee shirt all pushed up around her neck.

Puzzled, Joe asked, "What was that all about?"

She explained, "The egg timer's broken."

Rolling pin. Joe walked into the kitchen and his wife smacked him on top of his head with a rolling pin.

Joe said, "Honey? What was that for?!"

She said, "Well I was doing the laundry and I pulled out a piece of paper in your pocket with the name 'Billy Sue' written on it!"

"Honey, that's the name of a horse I got to bet on at the track." Joe's wife shrugs and walks away.

Three days later, Joe walks into the kitchen again and his wife smacks him in the head with a rolling pin. "Honey, what was that for?"

The wife said, "Your horse just called."

Bumpy Landing. The pilot of a 2-seater Cessna 152 was told by Ground Control to hold short of the active runway while a Boeing 747 landed. The 747 landed and then passed by the Cessna.

One of the 747 crew said over the radio, "Oh look at the tiny plane. Did you make that in your garage all by yourself?"

The Cessna pilot replied, "Yes, I did, and I made it out of 747 parts! I am going to go out on the runway and collect more parts after I saw the landing you just made."

Polygamous. A four-year-old boy after watching "The King and I" said to his Mom, "When I grow up, I'm going to have 5 wives, one who will cook, one who will wash, one who will clean up, one who will sing to me, and one who will go with me outside."

Mom replied, "Johnny, you also might want one to put you to sleep?"

"No mom, I will sleep with you."

A tear formed around Mom's eyes. "God bless you,

Johnny." Mom whispered, then said, "But who will sleep with our 5 wives?"

"Let them sleep with Daddy," Johnny said.

A tear formed in Dad's eye. "God bless you, my son."

Helpful suggestion. A guy was standing in a bar and a man sits down next to him. After a while, they get to talking and at about 10:00 pm the second man says,

"Oh well, I better get home. My wife doesn't like me to stay out late in the evening."

The first guy replies, "I'll help you out of this. I do this all the time when I'm out too late. Just do what I say. Go home and sneak into the bedroom. Get down and put your head between her legs then perform cunnilingus for about 20 minutes and there will be no complaints in the morning."

The man's not sure of whether to do this or not but nods his head agreeing and continues to drink for another hour before heading home to give it a try.

When he gets home, the house is pitch black. He sneaks upstairs into the bedroom, pulls back the covers and proceeds to perform cunnilingus for 20 minutes.

The bed is like a swamp. He decides to get up and wash his face.

As he walks into the bathroom, his wife is sitting on the toilet.

Seeing her, he screams, "What the hell are you doing in here?!"

"Quiet!", she says. "You'll wake my mother."

Singles bar. "I met my wife at a singles bar," Joe said.

"Really? I met my wife that way too."

"I don't think so," said Joe, "When I met my wife at the bar, she was supposed to be home with the kids."

Dictatorship. In Russia, there are only two TV channels. Channel One contains nothing but government propaganda.

On Channel Two, a uniformed KGB agent comes up on the screen and says, "Go back to Channel One!"

Are you tired of paying extra airline baggage fees? True story. In 2012, a man wore 60 shirts and nine pairs of jeans on an eleven-and-a-half-hour flight from China to Africa.

He did this since he didn't want to pay the extra baggage fee. It's hilarious, but most people do not recommend being a walking closet for yourself.

No respect. "When I was a kid, I got no respect. I told my mother, I'm gonna run away from home. She said, 'On your mark'. When my mother would put me in the sandbox to play, the cat kept trying to cover me up." -- Rodney Dangerfield

True Optimism. "I may be going to hell, but at least the dinners won't ever be served cold." -- Anon.

Don't worry. Be Happy! If a problem can be solved then there's no use worrying about it, but if a problem can't be solved then what's the use of worrying?

Play on words. A string walks into a bar and sits and says "Bartender, give me a scotch on the rocks!"

The bartender stares at him and says, looks at him and says, "What the hell? You are a string!

The string says, "Yes, I am a string."

"Well, you have to leave."

The next day…the string wants to have a beer and goes back to the bar, sits down and says to the bartender, "Give me a scotch on the rocks!" The bartender looks at him and says "I thought I told you yesterday, we don't serve your kind here. If I see you here again, I'm calling the cops!"

The string leaves, but still wants a beer. So, the string decides to wear a disguise. He ties himself up in a bunch of knots like a monkey's fist, but one last piece of string is sticking out and fuzzy.

The string goes back into the bar, sits down and says, "Bartender, give me a scotch on the rocks!"

The bartender stares at him and says, "Aren't you that string I've been kicking out of here?" that's been hanging around here lately?"

The string looks him straight in the eye and says, "No, I'm a frayed knot."

Hell! In southern Norway, there is a village named "Hell." Yes. Norway has 4 seasons and as you might have guessed every winter Hell freezes over!

What'd you call me? Joe was in a bad car accident and almost died. He recovered at the hospital, but he lost an eye, so they gave him a wooden eye until a glass eye could be made up.

Joe was depressed and didn't do much. His friends came around and persuaded him to go out to a bar to have some fun.

At the bar, Joe who was a good-looking man sat there staring at his beer. One of his friends said, "Hey look at that cute girl over there. Joe, go and ask her to dance."

"Nope, not me," Joe said. She wouldn't dance with me – a guy with a wooden eye."

"What about the girl over there?" His friend said.

"Oh no. She's okay but her nose – it's sadly out of proportion to her face. It's too big for me."

Joe continued looking around then got up and walked over to the girl with a large nose.

"Do you want to dance?" Joe asked.

The girl got very excited at being asked to dance by such a good-looking man and shouted, "Would I! Would I!"

Joe walked away saying, "Big nose! Big nose!"

First time. Joe got divorced and married Jane. This was Joe's second marriage and Jane's third.

On their wedding night, Jane said, "Joe, please be gentle."

"What?" Joe replied.

Jane looked at him shyly and said, "It's my first time."

Joe laughed, "You, a virgin? You've been married three times?"

Jane explained. "My first husband was a philosopher and he only talked about it."

"But your second husband was a doctor?"

"That's right," said Jane. "He was a gynecologist – he only looked at it. And my third husband was an engineer, and he took over a year to design a new way to do it."

"Why didn't you ever ask me about sex?" Joe asked.

"Well, I married you since I knew you were going to f*ck me just like you do to your constituents every day."

How poor were you? When I was a kid, I was so poor we used to visit my rich grandma in the poor house for the homeless.

We were so poor, every Christmas we got a piece of paper with the word "coal" written on it.

We were so poor we would open our junk mail to eat spam.

We were so poor when we went to KFC, we licked other people's fingers.

Be careful what you bet for. After losing a drunken poker bet in 2009, a New Zealand man had his name legally changed to,

"Full Metal Havok More Sexy N Intelligent Than Spock And All The Superheroes Combined With Frostnova."

It took five years, but the name was finally approved by the NZ government. All 99 characters of his new name are on his passport. [19] He and his wife, if there is one, and his children, if any, most likely will have a lot of laughs at roll calls.

Funny, crazy and highly imaginative, some probably want to party with this guy!

Prescriptions require full disclosure of possible side effects which makes taking drugs a bit dangerous. For example, Joe couldn't sleep so he went to the doctor for a prescription for sleeping pills.

When he read the label, the possible side effects were amnesia and paranoia.

Now, when Joe's wife asks him how he slept, he replies, "I don't remember how I slept and who sent you?"

Ouch! The preacher asked his congregation for someone to testify if their prayers were answered and a young woman raised her hand.

"Mrs. Jones, please tell us about it," the preacher asked.

"Several weeks ago, my husband fell off a ladder and crushed his scrotum. He was in terrible pain. Our doctor did the best he could but had to refer him to two more doctors. He was in so much pain, we had to help him around the house. He couldn't work and anytime he moved, he suffered so much pain."

She continued her story even though the men in the church started to shift uncomfortably listening to her.

"I prayed and prayed as my husband had to go through several operations. The doctors were able to put together the pieces of his scrotum and keep things in place with a strong metal wire."

A few groans were heard from the men in the congregation.

"Thanks to the prayers of our family, he is almost recovered but still has to take it very easy. But his scrotum should heal."

Her husband was sitting next to her and stood up and said, "Hi everyone, I'm her husband and I just want to say the correct word for my wife's story is sternum."

Remedy. A Patient consulted his doctor and told him he was sick and depressed. The doctor said, "You should cut down on drinks."

"But I don't touch a drop," the patient said.

"Then you should cut down on smoking."

"But I don't smoke."

"Then you should stop taking drugs."

The patient answered, "I don't do drugs."

"Then you should cut down on womanizing."

"I haven't chased women in my life."

The doctor paused then said, "In that case, go to bar and have a shot and beer, smoke a fine cigar and try some marijuana too. Then take a few girls home with you."

A thought just occurred to me. If I had spent the time doing the things, instead of procrastinating about them, I would have accomplished a hell of a lot more in my life.

Wow! That's profound. I'm going to lie down and think about that. And, if procrastination was a sport, I would compete in it later.

Leaving the intercom on. An Australian airline pilot forgot his intercom was on and told his copilot, "What I need now is a cold beer and a hot Sheila."

One of the lady flight attendants ran up the aisle to the cockpit to tell the pilots the intercom was on. As she rushed past, a lady passenger remarked, "Honey, don't forget the beer!"

Reincarnation.

* A young boy told an old man, "Yeah, well, I didn't believe in reincarnation when I was your age, either."

* You can always tell if a deceased person believed in reincarnation by looking at their tombstone. Instead of "Rest in Peace" or "RIP", you will see "BRB" or "Be Right Back."

* "Yes, well, there was a time when I believed in reincarnation, but that was many, many years ago – a very long time ago - in some other life." **-- Dave Schinbeckler**

Nancy Astor and Winston Churchill. When Nancy Astor, the first female member of Parliament told Winston Churchill he was disgustingly drunk, Winston replied, "My dear, you are ugly, but tomorrow I shall be sober, and you will still be ugly."

Nancy also told him that if she was married to him, she would poison his coffee.

Churchill replied, "Nancy, if you were my wife, I'd drink it."

Mice and the four churches. There were four churches in a small town, an Evangelical Church, a Baptist Church, a Church of the Latter-Day Saints, and a Catholic Church and all four churches were overrun with mice.

The Evangelical Church called a meeting to decide how to get rid of the mice. After much discussion and prayer, they decided the mice were put there by God and decided to do nothing so as not to interfere with God's will.

The Baptist Church officials decided to put the mice in the baptistery and drown them, but the mice sneaked out and afterward, there were three times the number of holy mice running around the Church.

The Church of the Latter-Day Saints decided they did not want to hurt God's creations, so they captured all the mice and drove them miles away and released them. Several days later, the mice came back and brought back more mice with them.

The Priests in the Catholic Church discussed and prayed what to do with the huge number of mice and after much prayer and deliberation, they decided to baptize all the mice as Catholics and make them parishioners of the Church. The mice now only visit the Church on Easter and Christmas.

Airline food. Tower: "United 222, you are cleared for takeoff, contact Departure on frequency 121.7."

United: "United 222 switching to Departure. We saw a dead animal near the far end of the runway after we lifted off."

"Tower (now talking to another plane): "Delta 121, cleared for takeoff behind United 222. Delta 121, did you copy that report about the dead animal?"

Delta 121: "Delta 121, roger; and yes, we copied, and we've already notified our caterers."

For real. "Gentleman, Chicolini here may look like an idiot and talk like an idiot, but don't let that fool you. He really is an idiot." **-- Groucho Marx in Duck Soup.**

What is better? Is it better to be an optimist or a pessimist?

"While those arseholes were arguing over whether the glass of beer was half-empty or half-full, I drank the beer. Call me an opportunist." -- Anon.

Government Investigation. Agents of a large State Department of Transportation Agency found over 200 dead crows on its highways recently, and there was concern that they may have died from an Asian Flu.

A Pathologist examined the remains of all the crows, and, to everyone's relief, confirmed the problem was NOT Asian Flu. The cause of death appeared to be from vehicular impacts. However, during analysis, it was noted that varying colors of paint appeared on the bird's beaks and claws.

By analyzing these paint residues, it was found that 98% of the crows had been killed by impact with motorbikes, while only 2% were killed by cars.

The Agency then hired an Ornithological Behaviorist to determine if there was a cause for the disproportionate percentages of motorbike kills versus car kills. The Ornithological Behaviorist quickly concluded that when crows eat roadkill, they always have a look-out crow to warn of danger. They discovered that while all the lookout crows could shout "Cah!", not even one could shout "bike."

Misdiagnosis. A wife was complaining about shortness of breath and her husband took her to the doctor. After meeting with the doctor, the wife told the husband her problem was she had attractive genitalia.

"What?" Her husband was outraged.

He barged in on the doctor and said, "What's this about you telling my wife she had attractive genitalia?"

"I didn't say that." Said the doctor. "I said she has acute angina."

Deer crossing. I live in a semi-rural area. We recently had a new neighbor call the local city council office to request the removal of the DEER CROSSING sign on our road.

The reason: "Too many deer are being hit by cars out here! I don't think this is a good place for them to be crossing anymore."

Riddles. "Someone told me once the ability to solve riddles shows a sane and logical mind. I enjoy riddles and take them seriously." **-- Stephen King**

Putting him down. "Lie down so I can recognize you," said boxer Willie Pep greeting a former opponent.

Castle conversation starters or stoppers. Spiral staircases in medieval castles run clockwise. This is because all knights used to be right-handed. When the intruding army would climb the stairs, they would not be able to use their right hand, since the right hand was holding the sword and there were the usual difficulties of climbing the spiral stairs.

But then you might think left-handed knights would have no trouble. But left-handed people could never become knights because they were assumed to be descendants of the devil.

Fun Riddles.

Q. What is it that you can hold but can't ever touch?

A. Your breath.

Q. What breaks yet never falls, and what falls yet never breaks?

A. Day and night

Q. If it takes 5 elves 5 minutes to make 5 dolls, then how long will it take 100 elves to make 100 dolls?

A. It takes 1 elf 5 minutes to make a doll, so it would take 100 elves 5 minutes to make 100 dolls.

Q. A doctor and a bus driver are both in love with the same woman, an attractive girl named Sarah. The bus driver had to go on a long bus trip that would last a week. Before he left, he gave Sarah seven apples. Why?

A. An apple a day keeps the doctor away!

Q. How many months in one year from January to December have 28 days?

A. All of them.

This is a hard one. Who entered their own look-alike contest and came in third place?

(Answer on p. 182)

Not complicated. Men complain about how complicated women are. My girlfriend is very simple to understand. She only wants two things. The first is faithfulness to her. She wants unwavering loyalty. And I have a look for any woman who tries to flirt with me that instantly makes the flirting stop.

The second thing my girlfriend wants is orgasms. Those are the only two things she wants.

Oh, wait, money. I've got to remember money.

A question of time. A customer asked an attractive single lady cashier at a bank if there was any change in interest depending on when he first made a deposit compared to when he withdraws.

The attractive lady cashier said, "Sir, interest doesn't depend on when you put in or when you take it out, it depends on how long it has been in."

Selling. Q. How do you know right away if someone can sell?

A. You hear things like,

"He could sell a parachute to Superman."

"He could sell a glass a water to a drowning man."

"He could sell a hairbrush to Vin Diesel, Yul Brenner, Gandhi, Michael Jordan and Mike Tyson and have them all fight over who is going to buy the first one."

"He could sell a ketchup Popsicle to a lady wearing white gloves and a white wedding dress on her way to the altar a hot day in July."

Christmases over time. You begin by believing in Santa Claus. As you grow older, you no longer believe in Santa Claus. Then you dress like Santa Claus in a red suit and a white beard. Finally, you look like Santa Claus.

Don't have names? When I was a kid in the 4th grade, I was asked to name all the presidents. Hey, all of the presidents already had a name!

High school teachers are very strict. They tell you again and again, "Don't drink alcohol, don't do any drugs, and don't be promiscuous and sleep with everyone. They tell you these things, so you can get good grades, graduate, and go to college where you can do all these.

Oranges. The police broke up a prostitution ring at an exclusive Florida Resort on a late summer afternoon and lined up 10 girls they just arrested outside on the driveway entrance to the resort.

The grandmother of one of the girls was going by slowly walking with her cane when she noticed her granddaughter standing in line.

"Why are you standing in line, my dear?" Grandma asked.

Not wanting to tell her grandma what was going on, she replied, "Grandma, the police are giving away free oranges and we are standing in line for them."

"Why that's awfully nice of them. I'd like to get some too, so I'll stand in line with you."

A policeman was going down the line asking each girl for identification and other details from all the prostitutes. When he got to Grandma he said,

"Wow, grandma! You still going at this at your age?"

Grandma smiled and said, "Oh, it's easy. I just take out my teeth and suck them dry."

Forgive their enemies. Joe decided to become a minister and loved to give sermons to his Sunday congregation. He talked one Sunday about forgiveness and preached on and on. He asked the congregation to raise their hands to find out how many in the congregation were willing to forgive their enemies.

Only a few of the congregation raised their hands. So, Joe went on longer preaching it is best in the eyes of God to forgive your enemies. After 20 minutes more of his preaching, he asked again for a show of hands. This time he got a show from 75% of the congregation.

So, Joe continued to preach forgiveness for another 20 minutes, then finally asked for a show of hands on how many were willing to forgive their enemies.

Everyone raised their hands except one little old woman seated in the back of the church.

Joe looked at her and said, "Why don't you want to forgive your enemies?"

"I don't have a single enemy," she said.

"Wow!" Joe said. "That's fantastic and may I ask your age?"

"I'm 99," Mrs. Smith replied.

"That's fantastic! In your 99 years, you don't have any enemies! Mrs. Smith, would you come up here and tell the congregation how you managed in your 99 years to not to have an enemy on this good earth?"

Mrs. Smith slowly went up the aisle to the front and then turned around to everyone and said, "I just outlived the f*ckin' b*tches."

True story. A very elderly grandmother finished shopping and was walking to her car in the parking lot when she noticed 4 young men getting into her car and trying to drive it away.

For protection, the elderly lady carried a handgun and when she saw the young men stealing her car, she dropped her bags and pulled out her handgun and started screaming, "Get away from my car! I've got a gun!"

The four young men turned and looked at her and saw her gun, then jumped out of the car and ran like hell.

The incident so shook the elderly woman, she couldn't get her key into the ignition. She kept fumbling and fumbling with her keys and couldn't start the car.

As she calmed down, she noticed a soccer ball, a baseball cap, and two six-packs of beer on the passenger seat next to her.

She got out and realized her car was parked 5 spaces down.

She went to the Police Station anyway and reported the incident to the desk sergeant who started laughing hysterically.

As the sergeant was trying to catch his breath, he pointed to 4 young men who had just come in to report a carjacking by a crazy old lady, who was waving a huge gun at them.

Why would you do this? Thomas Blackthorne set a new world record in 2022 by lifting 27 pounds using just his tongue.

He accomplished this after 6 years of training (6 years?). His tongue was pierced with a hook on it and successfully had no injury to himself.

New dating site. I've decided to launch a brand-new dating app exclusively for Paleontologists....... I'm going to call it "Carbon Dating".

Party games. "Be careful which party games you play. It would be very bad if you had a heart attack especially when playing charades." **-- Demetri Martin**

No smoking. Joe was smoking in a pharmacy and the counter girl told him, "Sorry, no smoking in the store, please."

Joe said, "Hey, why not? I bought this package of smokes here."

"Why? Well, we sell a lot of things in this store. Everything from prescriptions to prophylactics and just because we sell prophylactics, you can't start f*cking us!"

Say what? "I don't like "yes-men" working for me. I see their sign language, their body language always showing submission and agreement. I want anyone who works for me to tell the truth period. Being honest and talking honestly is the most important thing an employee can do, even if it costs them their job. " -- **Samuel Goldwyn**

Pedestrian light beeping. The pedestrian light on the corner beeps when it's safe to cross the street.

I was crossing with an 'intellectually challenged' coworker of mine.

He asked if I knew what the beeper was for.

I explained that it signals blind people when the light is red.

Appalled, he responded, 'What on earth are blind people doing driving?'

Wrong parts. Tarzan was in a bad fight with a lion. In that fight he had his arm torn off, his eye ripped out, and his penis torn off. So, to get help with his wounds he swung into his local witch doctor. The doctor saw he was in rough shape and went right to work to patch him up.

Since he was missing three different body parts, he had to find a solution to replace them all.

So first he put an eagle's eye in for his eye. Next, he used an ape arm for his severed arm. But when it came to replacing his penis, the doctor was very perplexed.

After deliberating a long time, the doctor exclaimed, "I've got it, I've got it! I'll give you an elephant trunk for your lower member."

The doctor patched him all up and sent him on his way telling Tarzan, "Make an appointment in two weeks for a follow up."

Tarzan swung back two weeks later.

The doctor asked. "How's the eagle's eye?"

"Great!" says Tarzan "I can see farther than ever."

The doctor asked, "How's the ape's arm?"

"Fantastic," says Tarzan. "I can lift so much more than I ever could before."

"Wow that's great!" said the doctor. "How's the elephant's trunk?"

"Well, Doc that's a different story, because every time I get hungry, it picks up a clump of grass and stuffs it up my arse."

Only Carlin. "Why is "abbreviation" such a long word?" – George Carlin

By the way, the technical name for the "fear of long words" is "hippopotomonstrosesquippedaliophobia." An amazing word as even pronouncing that word is a task. This is how it's pronounced, "Hi-poh-po-toh-mon-stroh-ses-kwee-peh-dah-leejoh-foh-beeja."

Free drinks. An English man, Irishman and a Scotsman are sitting in a crowded pub.

The Englishman said, "The pubs in England are the best. You can buy one drink and get one free".

Everyone in the pub agreed and gave a big cheer.

The Scotsman said, "That's fine, but in my country, you buy one drink and get two more free drinks." Again, the crowd in the pub gave a big cheer.

The Irishman said, "Ireland has the best pubs. In Ireland, you buy one drink, get another 3 drinks for free, and then they take you in a private room for a shag."

The Englishman says, "Wow! Did that happen to you?"

The Irishman replied, "No sir, it didn't happen to me. My sister told me that's what happened to her."

Wrong number. Joe picked up the phone and listened for two seconds then said, "Well, I don't know. Check the weather yourself!" Then Joe slammed the phone down.

"Who was it?' asks Josephine.

"Wrong number. It was some arsehole wanting to know if the coast was clear."

Is it dark here? "It's dark in here, isn't it?" One blonde said to the other blonde.

"I don't know; I can't see," said the other.

Keyboard. "My wife told me she'd slam my head into the keyboard if I don't get off the computer. I'm not too worried, I   think   she's   just joking............l34hgeoin,./gakljeojYTRDAo4iuds treisdns02]3 309[oewfm [o0irt0jed…"

Spontaneous. A husband and wife sit at home in the evening watching television.

The husband is drinking a glass of his favorite beer and the wife is drinking a glass of her favorite wine. "I love you," says the husband.

Surprised, the wife says, "Is that you or the beer talking?"

"This is me talking to the beer."

What bird is nicknamed the "Laughing Jackass"?

(Answer on p. 183)

Confusing text messages.

Joe received a text message:

"Sorry sir I am using your wife, day and night, when you are not at home. In fact, I use your wife much more than you do.

"I am feeling guilty, and I hope you will accept my sincere apology."

Joe was stunned until a second message was received shortly thereafter:

"Damn predictive text. I meant 'Wi-Fi.'"

Unfreezing. Joe's wife sent him a text on a cold winter evening: "Windows frozen."

Joe sent a text back, "Pour warm water over them."

A short time later, Joe got another text from his wife, "the laptop is completely f*cked up now."

Too Many Lawsuits. A man was having problems with his late-model luxury car as he drove through a high crime area at 2 am on a Saturday night. As he drove, he found his brakes were going and they eventually failed to work. He parked the car and called a taxi and left his car on the street, planning to get a tow truck the next day to tow it in for repairs.

A car thief stole the car shortly thereafter and drove it downhill into a tree resulting in the thief breaking vertebrae in his back. The thief had a permanent injury and filed a lawsuit against the car owner.

The lawyer for the car owner asked the judge to dismiss the ridiculous case. No one should profit from wrongdoing.

The thief's argument was that the car owner "should have known his car would be stolen" in a high crime area when he left it on the street at 2 am. He claimed all the car owners had to do was to leave a note on his car that it had no brakes.

The court held the thief had a valid case of negligence against the car owner for not reasonably foreseeing his car would be stolen and that someone would be injured trying to drive it away. He was therefore responsible if the thief could prove his allegations at trial.

Before the case went to trial, it was settled outside of court for an undisclosed sum.

What's a couple? "I asked my mom this question. She said, 'Two or three'. Which probably explains why her marriage collapsed." – **Josie Long**

Choices. "My psychologist told me to write a letter to people I hate then burn them. Did that but I don't know what to do with the letters."

Walked Into a Bar. After several days crossing the hot Arizona desert, a cowboy staggered into a town as thirsty as hell. He walked into the bar and was about to ask for a drink when a man dashed into the bar and yelled, "Big Joe is coming! Big Joe is coming!" Everyone in the bar jumped up out of their seats and ran out of the bar.

The thirsty man still wanted his drink but when he looked around everyone had left so he walked behind the bar and poured himself a beer.

Just then he heard huge loud hoofs pounding away on the street outside. A huge man was riding a wild buffalo down the street. He stopped in front of the bar, and tied the buffalo up. The ground shook as he stomped into the bar and tore the swinging doors off their hinges.

The huge man was the meanest and ugliest guy the cowboy had ever seen. The man slammed his fist on the bar cracking the top of the bar almost breaking the bar in half and said, "Give me whiskey! NOW!"

The cowboy grabbed a whiskey bottle and shakily began to pour a whiskey when the huge man grabbed the bottle and chugged all the whiskey down. Then he threw the empty bottle against the wall smashing it into a thousand pieces.

Then the gigantic man made a beeline toward the door.

The cowboy scratched his head and said, "You're leaving?"

The huge man turned around and said, "Hell yeah! Haven't you heard? Big Joe is coming! Big Joe is coming!"

Fast-thinking poodle. An eccentric little old woman hadn't ever seen Africa and decided to take a trip there and took her little poodle along with her. They were out on a safari and the little poodle wandered off and got lost in a dense jungle.

Trying to find his way back, the little poodle saw a huge lion rapidly approaching him.

The poodle starts to chew on bones on the ground and said as loud as he could, "Man that lion tasted great! Maybe I can find another lion to eat!"

Hearing this, the approaching lion ran away thinking "That was close! I was almost eaten by a poodle!"

A monkey saw all this going on and ran to tell the lion the poodle outsmarted him. The poodle saw the monkey running toward the lion but couldn't catch the monkey in time before the monkey told the lion the poodle made a fool out of him.

The angry lion told the monkey, "Hop on my back and watch me have that poodle for lunch."

The poodle saw the lion coming fast at him with a monkey on its back. The poodle yelled as loud as he could, "Where's that f*ckin monkey. I sent him off some time ago to get another lion for me!"

The tallest man in the world - ever. Robert Wadlow (aka the "Alton Giant" and "Giant of Illinois") grew to 8 feet, 11.1 inches tall in 1940. He was the tallest man who ever lived. [20]

He was born in 1918 and weighed only 8.7 pounds. However, he began growing at a rapid rate when he was a child due to hyperplasia of his pituitary gland (which wasn't ever treated).

It was reported he had to eat 8,000 calories a day to sustain himself and he sadly died at the young age of 22 and was still growing.

Irate airport ground control - true story. While taxiing at London's Heathrow Airport, the crew of a United flight departing for Miami made a wrong turn and came nose-to-nose with a Continental 727 airliner.

The lady controller lost it and strongly lectured the UA shouting, "United 3771, where the HELL are you going!? I told you to turn left on Alpha taxiway! You turned right on Charlie! Stop right there! Goddamnit! You don't even know your alphabet! Get it right!"

She didn't stop there and continued her rage at the embarrassed crew and shouted almost hysterically, "God! Now you've messed it all up and screwed it all up way more than you know! You stay put! Don't you move a millimeter! You will get further instructions in half an hour and in the meantime, you stay right there! You got that, United 3771!?"

"Yes, we do ma'am," one of the humbled crew replied.

The ground communications fell silent after the verbal tirade of the United crew. Others listening were giving the ground controller time to calm down.

After a long silence, an anonymous pilot pierced the silence and said, "You're one of my ex-wives, aren't you?"

Be careful what you wish for. Three guys on a deserted island in the middle of the ocean find a magic lantern. They rub it and a genie pops out and granted each of them one wish.

156

The first guy said, "Get me off this island and get me home." In an instant, he was gone."

The second guy wished the same and likewise disappeared.

The third guy said, "Hey! It's lonely here. I wish to have my friends back here."

Thrifty Joe. Penny-pinching Joe and his wife were at the county fair and saw an exhibit for a biplane ride for $95 per person but Joe thought that was too much for a short ride. So, he bargained with the pilot and offered him $95 as the total price to take them both up.

The aerobatic pilot was reluctant to bargain but business had been slow, so he said, "Okay, I'll take you both up for $95. But if you scream, shout or say anything, you pay me double - $95 for each of you."

Joe talked it over with his wife and they agreed and got into the plane sitting tandem behind the pilot. The pilot soared up steeply into the sky. Then he went into a steep dive followed by loops, barrel rolls, and flew inverted along with other very thrilling aerobatic maneuvers.

As they were coming in for the final landing, the pilot remarked, "You two were amazing! You didn't say a word!"

Joe replied, "I almost did when my wife fell out."

The airline passenger and the parrot. Joe took his seat on the plane and was surprised to find a beautiful colored Macaw parrot all by itself in the seat next to him. The flight took off and after the seat belt light went out, the flight attendant walked past them.

The parrot shouted out, "Hey, You! You're an ugly lazy good for nothing! Dammit! Get me a double scotch and I want it now!" The flight attendant scowled at the bird and continued walking.

A few moments later she walked past again, and the parrot squawked, "I said to hurry your stinking butt and get me that scotch! Now!"

The flight attendant got extremely angry but returned with a scotch for the parrot.

Joe who wasn't too bright assumed this was a great way to get a quick drink too, so he said, "Hey lady! I want a scotch and make it snappy! Yeah, that's right! I want it now!" Joe went on and on and continued demanding a scotch!

The flight attendant couldn't take it anymore and immediately went to the front of the plane. She returned with a huge security man and a big male flight attendant who grabbed Joe and the parrot and lifted them out of their seats. Then walked them to the back and threw both out of the plane at 10,000 feet!

As Joe and the parrot were hurled out the back door, the parrot remarked, "For someone who can't fly, you've got a lotta balls!"

Your neighbor's cow. What is illegal to put on your neighbor's cow in Texas?

(Answer on p. 183)

Only one requirement. From the Congressional Cemetery's FAQs on its website:

Q. Do you have to be a Member of Congress (or any other requirement) to be buried there?

A. No. You just have to be dead.

Red Beans and Rice. Red Beans and Rice are a New Orleans classic dish. They are best eaten on Mondays since years ago, women would do laundry on Mondays and red beans would cook all day without needing much attention. They were usually cooked and seasoned with a leftover hambone from Sunday night's dinner.

An old man in New Orleans walked into a grocery store and asked a boy who was stocking shelves if he could buy a half a can of red beans and half a bag of rice. The boy told him that they sell only full cans of beans and full bags of rice. But the old man insisted and requested the boy to ask his boss.

The boy walked into the back and asked his boss, "Some cheap, crazy old asshole wants to buy a half a can of red beans and a half a bag of rice." The boss frowned. The boy turned around and saw the old man standing behind him. The boy continued, "and this very fine gentleman was kind enough to buy the other half can and half bag."

The boss told the boy to get the man a half a can of red beans and half a bag of rice and told him later, "You are a quick thinker, and we need more quick-thinking people like you working here. Where are you from, boy?"

"I'm from Texas, sir," the boy replied.

"Why did you leave Texas?" The boss asked.

"Sir, there's nothing there but prostitutes and rodeo people in Texas."

"Oh, is that so?" The boss replied. "My wife is from Texas."

"Really? What rodeo is she with?"

Bringing out the best in others and ourselves. "When we seek to discover the best in others, we somehow bring out the best in ourselves." **-- William Arthur Ward**

Airline puns.

- He bought an old plane and made it into a posh restaurant. I don't think it will take off.
- I'm getting tired of all the arguments and controversy over unmanned aircraft. It's just droning on and on.
- A retired lawyer worked as a baggage handler but was let go since he kept losing cases.
- To everyone's surprise, out of the blue, he became a skydiver.
- "Things are looking up!" Orville Wright said to his brother, Wilbur, after their first flight.
- The temperature of the coffee is inversely proportional to the time and strength of turbulence.

Unintended Compliment. A husband and wife are watching the evening news. The news team was discussing a beautiful movie star's engagement with an obnoxious, rude, loudmouthed world champion wrestler.

Husband: "I just can't believe that! Why do the most self-centered, opinionated, egotistical, and cynical a-holes in the world marry the most beautiful women?"

Wife: "Why thank you!"

The Deaf Yorkie. Our Yorkshire Terrier had trouble hearing so the wife took it to the vet. The vet said the dog's hearing was fine, but he had trouble hearing because there was too much hair in its ears. The vet cleaned the ears and clipped back a large amount of hair and the dog could then hear fine.

The vet suggested an easy way for her to prevent this in the future is to rub hair remover on her dog's ears once a month.

She went to the pharmacy and found a tube of hair remover and brought it to the register. The pharmacist advised her, "If you use this under your arms, you should avoid using deodorant for a day or two."

"But I'm not using it under my arms."

The pharmacist replied, "If you're using it on your legs, don't use body lotion for a day or two."

"But I'm not using it on my legs either. I'm using it on my Yorkie."

The pharmacist replied, "Well, don't ride your bike for about a week."

The Gentle Bully. Goliath was a gigantic bully who threatened the Jewish people. Actually, he was a gentile bully.

PT and a Bully. What is the difference between a personal trainer and a bully?

Nothing. They both beat you up and take your money.

Magazine ad. A popular magazine had a small ad toward the back which read,

"How you can get thousands of people to send you $2! A proven method that actually works! Send $2 with your email address to…"

A comedian gives it his best shot. A comedian tried his best to get his audience to laugh at one of his jokes. In desperation, he said, "I'm going to tell you 10 jokes – and they are the best puns I know – and whether you like it or not one of you is going to burst out in laughter."

After telling his 10 jokes, no pun in 10 did.

Suspicious Politician. A very influential politician began an affair with a well-known supermodel which went on for two months. He decided he was going to ask her to marry him but before doing so he asked his aides to anonymously hire a private detective to investigate her to see if she had previous affairs with other men.

Later the politician was given the private detective's report:

"She has a wonderful reputation and has great character. Her past is spotless and her family and friends all respect her very much. But for the past two months, she's been seen with a politician with a suspicious and untrustworthy background."

Big diamond. The world's largest diamond was found in the Premier Diamond Mine in Cullinan, South Africa in 2005. It is known as the Cullinan Diamond.

It weighed 3106.75 carats (1 pound 6 oz.!) and is worth around $400 million.

As far as is known it is the largest diamond ever found.

A Career in Politics. A man waited in a dark alley to mug someone. After a while, another guy walked down the same dark alley. The man jumped out, "Hey! Hey You!"

The other man said, "What the hell? What's with you?!"

"I like to intimidate people," the first man replied.

"Well," said the second guy, "I'll help you intimidate people if I can also shove 'em around a little."

"Sure, let's do it!"

The two men waited in the alley together when a third guy walked through. The two compatriots jumped out and moved forward menacingly. The third guy said, "Hold up, guys, it looks like you want to hurt me. How about we all work together and mug anyone who comes through? No one can stop all three of us!"

The first two agreed.

All three men are now waiting in the alley when a man dressed in a full suit and tie walked through. The three men jump out to ambush him and the man says, "Wait right there, my good sirs! How would you like an opportunity to join my group, where we intimidate, bully, and steal from anyone we want, then smile and deny it ever happened?"

The three men liked that and asked, "What group is that?"

The politicians!

164

Toilet paper color. What is the most popular color of toilet paper in France?

(Answer on p. 183)

Dating. After several weeks of trying, Joe finally got a beautiful co-worker to go out on a date with him. Joe spared no expense wanting to impress this beautiful woman and hired a limo, dressed up sharply and brought her to the most expensive restaurant in town.

However, she was not impressed, and Joe realized she was out of his league and the conversation dwindled during a very expensive dinner. Joe could tell she knew she was out of his league too. He excused himself and went to the restroom, but on his way there, he saw beautiful actress, Cate Blanchett sitting with a group of friends. This gave Joe an idea.

"Ms. Blanchett, I'm very sorry to interrupt you but I thought you might help me in a matter of the heart?" The waiter came over, but Cate waved him off and said, "For a matter of the heart, I would love to. How can I help you?"

"See that beautiful woman at that table. See that woman at that table? I've been lovestruck with her ever since I first saw her. But this is our first date, and nothing is going right. Would you kindly stop by our table and pretend to know me and treat me like an old friend? She's a big fan of yours and it would catapult me to the top of her list, for sure!"

Cate laughed and said, "Sure, why not? Go and sit down and I'll catch her eye and notice you and head straight over to you." Joe couldn't thank her enough and made the trip back to his table. As soon as he sat down, he heard Cate shout, "Joe! Is that you?"

Joe's date looked up and said, "God! Is that Cate Blanchett!"

Joe nodded it was.

"Joe, where on earth have you been?! I missed you so much! How long has it been?" Cate said as she approached their table.

Joe waved her off and said, "Listen, you crazy woman! I told you before we're not getting back together! Now you get out of here!"

Minimum wage. "I used to work at McDonald's making minimum wage.

"Do you know what that means when someone pays you minimum wage?

"Do you know what your boss was trying to say? 'Hey, if I could pay you less, I would, but it's against the law.'" **– Chris Rock**

True love? "Love is like a fart. If you have to force it, it's probably sh*t." **– Stephen K. Amos**

Settling the score. If someone (let's call him "Joe Doe") at a party is picking on you or ridiculing you, tell this joke.

Three lifelong friends recently found out they each suffer from incurable cancer, and they only have six months to live. They gather and decide they want to do something for which they will be remembered.

After thinking about it, the first man says, "I know. Let's see if we can get into the Guinness book of world records. All my life, I've been told I've got very long arms – maybe even the longest in the world! I'm going to send photos and data about my arms and see what they say."

The second man says, "Well, my nose is very big as you all know. Maybe I've got the biggest nose in the world. I'm going to send photos and data about my nose and see what happens too!"

The third man was still thinking and then finally said, "I'm sad to say this, but I've got a small penis. Perhaps the smallest penis in the world. I'm going to send photos and data on my penis to them!"

So, they all sent photos and data on their body parts along with notarized and witness affidavits and after several weeks they gather again when the latest edition of the Guinness Book of World Records came out.

The first man nervously opens the book and after reading about arms, jumps up and says, "Hey! I made it! I am the person with the longest arms in the world!"

The second man also very nervous, takes the book, looks up noses and shouts, "Hey! I've made it too! I am the person with the biggest nose in the world!" He turns to the first man and says, "We are now part of history!"

The third man takes the book and reluctantly looks up penises. He reads a bit, then shouts out, "Who the hell is Joe Doe?"

Eskimos. Two Eskimos sitting in a kayak were chilly. But when they lit a fire in the craft, it sank, proving once and for all that you can't have your kayak and heat it too.

Keys locked inside. When my wife and I arrived at a car dealership to pick up our car after a service, we were told the keys had been locked in it. We went to the service department and found a mechanic working feverishly to unlock the driver's side door.

As I watched from the passenger side, I instinctively tried the door handle and discovered that it was unlocked.

"Hey," I announced to the technician, "It's open!"

His reply was, "I know. I already did that side."

The Loving Frenchman. A Swiss, an Italian and a Frenchman were seated next to each other on a flight. After a few drinks, they started discussing their sex lives.

"Last night I made love to my wife four times," the Swiss said and this morning she made me delicious breakfast and she told me how much she adored me."

"Ah, last night I made love to my wife six times," the Italian said, "And this morning she made me a wonderful omelet and told me she could never love another man."

The Frenchman remained silent until he was asked, "And how many times did you make love to your wife last night?"

"Once," he replied.

"Only once?" the Italian arrogantly asked. "And what did she say to you this morning?"

"Don't stop," replied the Frenchman.

Be sure it's the correct move. I was having dinner with Magnus Carlsen, the current world chess champion, and we had a checkered tablecloth.

It took him two hours to pass me the salt.

One for the kids. What is Scooby Doo's full name?

(Answer on p. 183)

The most important things. John was away on a trip and after playing golf he was in the bar having a drink. His phone rings.

"Hello, Senor John? This is Juan the gardener."

"Ah yes, Juan. What's up?"

"I wanted to call you Senor to let you know your parrot has died."

"Oh no! Not my special parrot? Died? The one that could talk in two languages?"

"Si, Senor, your special parrot died."

"Shit! That's terrible! I'm going to miss that bird. How did it die?"

"It ate rotten meat, Senor."

"Rotten meat? How did it ever eat rotten meat?"

"From a dead horse, and he ate the meat of it."

"Dead horse? Where did the dead horse come from?"

"Your racehorse, Senor. It died from pulling the water cart all morning."

"What the hell are you talking about? Why is my prize racehorse pulling a cart carrying water?"

"We needed the water to put out the big fire."

"What the f*ck! What the hell happened over there? There was a fire?"

"A large fire happened at your house. The living room caught fire when a candle fell over."

"We have electric lights. Who was using a candle?"

"The candle was for the funeral, Senor."

"What the hell are you talking about?! What funeral!"

"Your wife's, Senor...she died. She came home very late and since no one tries to get in the house that late, I thought she was trying to break in, and I had to defend your home and I hit her with your new Driver."

Silence...

"Juan, if you even scratched that driver, you're fired!"

Acronyms. Wife: "How would you describe me?"

Husband: "ABCDEFGHIJK."

Wife: "What does that mean?"

Husband: "Adorable, beautiful, cute, delightful, elegant, fashionable, gorgeous, and hot."

Wife: "Aw, thank you, but what about IJK?"

Husband: "I'm just kidding!"

Q. Sometimes rescuing someone can be illegal. True or false?

A. Believe it or not, in St. Louis, Missouri, there is an old law still on the books (although not enforced) making it illegal for a firefighter to rescue a woman who is nude or if she is wearing a nightgown. [21]

The New Brain. A man walks into a brain store to buy a new brain. He goes to the clerk and says, "Hello, I'd like to purchase a new brain."

The clerk says, "Sure, here are some of our brains we have on sale. Here's the brain of a theoretical physicist, 5 dollars. This is on a special deal today.

"Here's our second deal for today. The brain of a what most people refer to as a "know it all" or you know, the guy or gal who always has to be right? Talks all the time – mostly about themselves. It's top of the line and sells for $10,000 dollars."

The man is now completely confused, and asks "Why is the brain of the know it all more expensive than of a physicist?"

"That's because it's never been used!" The clerk replies.

How Canada got its name. No one is sure but it is likely the name "Canada" comes from the Huron-Iroquois word "kanata," meaning "village" or "settlement."

In 1535, two Aboriginal youths told French explorer Jacques Cartier about the route to Kanata; they were referring to the village of Stadacona, the site of the present-day City of Québec. For lack of another name, Cartier used the word "Canada" to describe not only the village but also the entire area controlled by its chief, Donnacona.

But many say the Premiers of each of the new providences of Canada held a meeting to decide on a name for the entire country.

They held long meetings and went back and forth but there was no agreement on what to call the country. So, they decided to take all the letters in the alphabet and put them in a hat and draw the letters "oot" to see if they could come up with a name.

The chairman of the meeting began drawing the names out of the hat in front of them and announced them as he drew them out, "C eh? ... N eh? ... D eh?"

Punctuation. I'm giving up drinking for a month.

Sorry, that came out wrong.

I meant to write, "I'm giving up. Drinking for a month."

Holiday joke. A group of chess fanatics were just checking into a hotel and gathered together. Many were talking about their recent victories, intimidating the others as much as they could trying to get in their heads.

They talked on and on trying to one-up each other in their loud conversations.

After about an hour, the manager came out of the office and asked them to disperse.

"But why?" they asked, as they began to move off.

"Because" the manager replied, "I can't stand chess nuts boasting in an open foyer."

The pill worked too well! A lady goes to the doctor and complains that her husband is losing interest in sex. The doctor gives her a pill, but warns her that it's still experimental and tells her to slip it into his mashed potatoes at dinner.

That night, she does just that.

About a week later, she's back at the doctor, where she says, "Doc, the pill worked great! I put it in the potatoes like you said! It wasn't five minutes later that he jumped up, raked all the food and dishes onto the floor, grabbed me, and we had the most passionate sex ever there on the table!

The doctor says, "I'm sorry, we didn't realize the pill was that strong! The foundation will be glad to pay for any damages."

"Nah," she says, "that's okay. We're never going back to that restaurant anyway."

Humor and Advertising. It's been said many times laughter has a way of healing a lot of hurt feelings. A positive person laughs to forget while a negative person, more than not, forgets to laugh.

Well-known author, Grenville Kaiser believes humor is good for the mind and body. It's the best remedy for anxiety, depression, and negativity and it is a business asset. Good humor attracts people and will lead you to serenity and contentment.

The late David Ogilvy was known as the Father of Advertising and accomplished great things. He believed, "The best advertising ideas come as jokes. Make your thinking as funny as possible."

An old one. We all get older. There was an elderly couple who in their old age noticed that they were getting a lot more forgetful, so they decided to go to the doctor.

The doctor told them that they should start writing things down, so they don't forget.

They went home and the elderly lady told her husband to get her a bowl of ice cream. "You might want to write it down," she said.

The husband replied, "No, I can remember that you want a bowl of ice cream."

She then told her husband she wanted a bowl of ice cream with whipped cream. "Write it down," she told him again.

"No, no, I can remember you want a bowl of ice cream with whipped cream."

Then the lady said she wants a bowl of ice cream with whipped cream and a cherry on top. "Write it down," she told her husband.

"No, I got it. You want a bowl of ice cream with whipped cream and a cherry on top."

So, he goes to get the ice cream and spends an unusually long time in the kitchen, over 30 minutes. He comes out to his wife and hands her a plate of eggs and bacon.

The wife stares at the plate for a moment, then looks at her husband and asks, "Where's the toast?"

Donkey race. A Pastor entered his donkey in a race, and it won. The Pastor was so pleased with the donkey that he entered it into the race again and it won again.

The local paper read: PASTOR'S ASS OUT FRONT.

The bishop was so upset with this kind of publicity that he ordered the Pastor not to enter the donkey in another race.

The next day the local paper headline read: BISHOP SCRATCHES PASTOR'S ASS.

This was too much for the bishop, so he ordered the Pastor to get rid of the donkey. So, the Pastor decided to give it to a nun in a nearby convent.

The local paper, hearing of the news, posted the following headline the next day: NUN HAS BEST ASS IN TOWN.

The bishop fainted.

He informed the nun that she would have to get rid of the donkey, so she sold it to a farm for $10.

The next day the paper read: NUN SELLS ASS FOR $10.

This was too much for the bishop so he ordered the nun to buy back the donkey and lead it to the plains where it could run wild.

The next day the headlines read: NUN ANNOUNCES HER ASS IS WILD AND FREE.

The bishop was buried the next day.

The moral of the story is . . . being concerned about public opinion can bring you much grief and misery and even shorten your life. So be yourself and enjoy life.

Stop worrying about everyone else's ass and just cover your own! You'll be a lot happier and live longer!
Why wait? Whenever you get angry don't move, just stand there and start counting back from 10 to 1 aloud. Throw a punch at 3 since you'll usually catch him off guard.

Getting even. Joe lost all his money in Las Vegas and all he had left was his return airline ticket. He had to get to the airport. He waved down a cab. He told the cab driver he wanted to go to the airport.

The cab driver replied, "Oh you want to go to the airport. Hell, I was just going there without a passenger. You made my day. By the way, the fare is $25."

Joe said, "Look, I just lost everything I had on me, and I just need to get to the airport to return home. I'm good for $25 and I'll send you $50 if you just drive me to the airport. Here, write down my I.D. information. I'm good for the $25."

But the cab driver refused. "Look, buddy, either you got $25 cash or get the hell out!" Joe left and hitchhiked to the airport and eventually made it home.

A month later, Joe returned to Vegas, but this time he won a lot of money. As he was leaving for the airport, he noticed the cab driver who refused to take him to the airport the last time when he had no money was sitting at the end of a long cab line. There were twenty cabs in front of him.

Joe decided to get even and have some fun. He got into the first cab in the line and said, "How much to take me to the airport?"

"$25 dollars," said the first cab driver in line.

Joe continued, "And how much to give me a BJ on the way to the airport?"

The first cab driver told Joe to get the hell out of his cab.

So, Joe got in the next cab and asked the same two questions, and so on and all drivers refused until Joe got to the last cab.

When Joe got in the cab of the driver who refused to take him last year when he had no money, he said, "How much to take me to the airport?"

"$25," said the cab driver. "But why did those other drivers not take you?"

"I really don't know, they just said, they didn't want to go to the airport. Hey, here's $25 in advance. By the way, drive slowly by these drivers in line, so I can show them you were the one who is taking me to the airport?

The cab driver did this and as they passed the other cab drivers in line, Joe rolled down his window and smiled at every driver giving a thumbs up.

George isn't dumb. George, who had done very well for himself financially, is 79 years old and a member of an exclusive business club.

He walked into the club restaurant one evening with a gorgeous 22-year-old girl. She was an absolutely striking blonde on his arm.

They walked through the restaurant turning everyone's head along the way and sat down at a table amongst friends and the conversation was going well.

The amazing blonde excused herself to the restroom and got up and left the table.

"George! How the hell did you find a woman like that? Did you tell her you were 59?" his friend asked.

"God, no," George replied. "I told her I was 99."

Generous. The more generous we are, the more joyous we become.

The more cooperative we are, the more valuable we become.

The more enthusiastic we are, the more productive we become.

The more serving we are, the more prosperous we become.

-- William Arthur Ward

"Life is very short, so break your silly egos, forgive quickly, believe slowly, love truly, laugh loudly, and don't avoid things that make you smile." – **Ovilia**

"If you want to make the world a better place, be trustworthy, and respect people who are trustworthy.

"Be a friend and choose worthy friends.

"Don't tell a joke which might hurt someone. Don't laugh when someone else tells a joke that hurts someone.

"Being true to yourself is good for everyone around you since it gives them an example to be thoughtful as well. You will be loved for it, and you will influence others."

- Russ Roberts, American Author

Answers to Quiz Questions.

- **You can sneeze in your sleep. True or False?** *A. False.*

- **What was banned in Indonesia for stimulating passion?** *A. Hula Hoops*
  .

- **A guy fell off a 50-foot ladder but didn't get hurt. How come?** *A. He fell off the bottom step.*

- **Can you get arrested in Missouri for having your children take out the trash?** *A. In the State of Missouri, if your trash should have a beer can or empty bottle, it is illegal for a child to have it under his or her control – even if the can or bottle is empty. It comes under the illegal possession of alcohol, but the law is seldom enforced.*

- **Mac and Cheese. What country eats more macaroni and cheese than any other country in the world per capita?** *A. Canada.* [22]

- **Test the "Know-it-all.** Ask them if there is any word in the English language that rhymes with the word, "Month." *A. Sorry. There is no word in the English language that rhymes with the word, "Month".*

- **Who entered their own look-alike contest and came in third place?** *A. Charlie Chaplin*

- **What bird is nicknamed the "Laughing Jackass"?** *A. Kookaburra.*

- **What is illegal to put on your neighbor's cow in Texas?** *A. Graffiti.*

- **What is the most popular color of toilet paper in France?** *A. Pink.*

- **What is Scooby Doo's full name?** *A. Scoobert Doo.*

By the way. Try this. It's hilarious. There are some things in this world your brain cannot handle.

1. Sitting in a chair, lift your right foot off the floor and make clockwise circles.

2. Now, while doing this, draw the number 6 in the air with your right hand. Your foot will change direction.

There is nothing you can do to prevent this. It is entirely stupid, but you know you are going to try it again before the day is done if you haven't done so already!

Thank you for choosing this book! We hope you enjoyed it!

If you liked our book, we would sincerely appreciate your taking a few moments to leave a brief review.

Thank you again very much!

TeamGolfwell and Bruce Miller

Bruce@TeamGolfwell.com

About the authors

Bruce Miller. Lawyer, businessman, world traveler, golf enthusiast, Golf Rules Official, private pilot, TVC actor, and author of over 50 books, a few being Amazon bestsellers, spends his days writing, studying, and constantly learning of the astounding, unexpected, and amazing events happening in the world today while exploring the brighter side of life. He is a member of Team Golfwell, Authors, and Publishers.

TeamGolfwell are bestselling authors and founders of the very popular 300,000+ member Facebook Group "Golf Jokes and Stories." Their books have sold thousands of copies including several #1 bestsellers in Golf Coaching, Sports humor, and other categories.

We Want to Hear from You!

"There usually is a way to do things better and there is opportunity when you find it." - *Thomas Edison*

We love to hear your thoughts and suggestions on anything and please feel free to contact us at Bruce@TeamGolfwell.com

If you like golf, we invite you to join our 300,000+ member Facebook group, "Golf Jokes and Stories" – it's funny! [23]

Other Books by Bruce Miller [24] and Team Golfwell [25]

Brilliant Screen-Free Stuff to Do with Kids: A Handy Reference for Parents & Grandparents!

For the Golfer Who Has Everything: A Funny Golf Book

The Funniest Quotations to Brighten Every Day: Brilliant, Inspiring, and Hilarious Thoughts from Great Minds

For a Great Fisherman Who Has Everything: A Funny Book for Fishermen

And many more…

Index

Introduction iv

Screwdriver.. 1

Engineers 1

A baby is coming!... 3

Scotsman splurge... 3

How Many? 4

Quiz Question 4

Today is really unusual... 4

Aging... 4

Danger. 4

Things haven't changed much 5

The doctor and the old man 5

Choices 7

A few fun conversation starters. 8

Happy birthday 8

Fishing 8

Expressway to heaven.. 9

Honest people 10

Full-service counseling... 10

Ever want to get away from it all? 11

New truck 11

Getting Stronger Over the Years? 13

Eyebrows 13

Unexpected understatement 13

Forgetting things? 14

Oh, never mind 14

Operation 14

Female NFL 16

You get what you pay for 16

Sad, but as I get older, I think differently 16

So how cold was it? 16

Heaven or hell? 17

Keys locked inside 19

Lineman v. Backs 19

Job Interview. 19

Just in case you want to know. 20

Snow White 20

Negotiating 21

If you think your life is boring 21

Word choice..22

Mountain pun...22

Exercise for Seniors...22

Caribou..23

Fitness...23

Impossible...23

Q. Should I really have to touch my toes? 24

Accents 24

Caution grim humor...24

Saving up 26

Old is new again 26

Champagne? 27

Won the dance contest..27

Dramatic send-off..27

To avoid tears, stick it in the freezer for 15 minutes....30

Realization 30

Stairs...31

Coming in second 31

Not religious. 31

Thanks Doctor! 31

Revenge. 32

Getting married 32

Signing a cast 34

5 o'clock 34

Darwin was unusual 35

Pulled over 35

Get a loaf of bread 35

The Priest and the Rabbi 36

Wilson 37

Girl talk 37

Avoid eating beans. 37

Appropriately named 38

Ethical Issues. 38

Tough landing 38

Slinky 39

Say again? 39

Humbling 40

Quick thinking 40

Legal search? 41

Faking it 42

Another old one 42

Intercom..43

Speaks every seven years...44

What is the flavor?...45

What's that name? 45

You might have heard this one. 46

Tossing dwarfs...46

The traffic true test 46

Innocent 47

No thank you 47

Can I have a cookie?..48

Okaaay…...49

Small difference...49

Double-edged 49

Senior flight attendants. 50

Choices 50

What it takes. 51

Lose yourself...51

Just waiting...52

True Story..53

Dichotomy 55

Double-edged sword 55

Another true story 55

No job for you 55

Transferred to Texas 56

Long airport departure lines 57

Banned in Indonesia 57

The inquiring minds of kids 57

Last request 58

There's a lot here! 58

Arthritis. 59

The Brown Bomber 59

Medical exam 60

No more wandering 60

Lateral thinking 61

Real golf term meanings 61

Getting even 62

Expected outcome 63

Short of dinners. 63

Frugal and a healthy diet 64

Running late..66

Being absolutely clear...66

Comedians love Los Angeles 67

Choice of words...67

An old one you might not have heard. 67

Not sure yet..69

An airline is a requirement...69

Super quick thinking...70

A book title 3,777 words long?...70

Why is it?..70

She's tough. 71

Trash arrest. 72

Elephant..72

Arguments 73

Long line...73

Talking peanuts..74

Some are good and some are bad.....................................74

Fly pun..76

Light eater...76

Great carpentry 76

194

Accident...77

No bathtubs for donkeys. 77

Clever 78

Discrimination 78

True story..79

Bargaining 79

Calculations 80

If you must borrow 81

Translation..81

Legal business 81

The nature of a consultant..82

Chicago...82

If I had a nickel for every... 82

Need some sleep 83

Can singing be illegal?...84

Searching..84

Lose weight. 84

Elephant..85

No smoking on this airline..86

The engineer and the doctor..86

195

Indian land 87

Advice 87

Easy to spot the difference in engineers....................88

Chinese are great drivers 88

Hans? 89

Give me that bat! 90

Birthday 91

Cockpit talk. 92

Intruders..92

Accident...93

Explanation time...94

Borneo Roulette..95

Stopping a fight 96

69..96

Perception. 98

Want 10 more years? 98

Blinking...99

Well-oiled...99

Trivia to tell a secretary or typist 101

The shortest sentence 101

No heaven 101

Mac and Cheese 102

Wedding night 102

Lucky 102

Little-known basketball court 103

Pompous 103

The Laughing Captain 103

Test the "Know it all" 104

Excuse me 104

Every night 105

Let's add that again 105

An old one. 105

Old habits 106

Jet name 107

Trivia for fine dining. 107

Best restaurant. 107

The confession 108

An old one 109

Engineering students with time on their hands 109

You might not ever use this word 109

Model husband 110

Crystal ball.. 112

The phone call. 113

Viagra in a vase 114

Morning talk 114

Jealous 115

What's the point?.. 116

Busted 116

What town in America had a population of one?................................ 116

Don't have to say it... 117

Kite flying... 117

More conversation starters... 118

Club membership requirements. 118

Efficient 120

The usual 121

Rolling pin 121

Bumpy Landing 122

Polygamous. 122

Helpful suggestion. 123

Singles bar 124

Dictatorship 125

Are you tired of paying extra airline baggage fees 125

No respect... 125

True Optimism.. 125

Don't worry. Be Happy! 126

Play on words 126

Hell!.. 127

What'd you call me?.. 127

First time... 128

How poor were you?.. 129

Be careful what you bet for.. 129

Prescriptions 130

Ouch!.. 130

Remedy.. 131

A thought just occurred to me... 132

Leaving the intercom on. 132

Nancy Astor and Winston Churchill... 133

Mice and the four churches.. 134

Airline food. 135

For real 135

199

What is better? 135

Government Investigation 136

Misdiagnosis 137

Deer crossing. 137

Riddles. 137

Putting him down 138

Castle conversation starters or stoppers 138

Fun Riddles 138

Not complicated 139

A question of time 140

Selling 140

Christmases over time 141

Don't have names? 141

High school teachers 141

Oranges 142

Forgive their enemies. 142

True story 144

Why would you do this? 145

New dating site 145

Party games 145

No smoking 146

Say what?... 146

Pedestrian light beeping.. 146

Wrong parts 147

Only Carlin 148

Free drinks 148

Wrong number... 149

Is it dark here? 149

Keyboard 149

Spontaneous.. 150

Confusing text messages.. 150

Unfreezing 151

Too Many Lawsuits 151

What's a couple? 152

Choices 152

Walked Into a Bar... 152

Fast-thinking poodle 153

The tallest man in the world - ever 155

Irate airport ground control - true story 156

Be careful what you wish for.. 156

Thrifty Joe 157

The airline passenger and the parrot 157

Your neighbor's cow 158

Only one requirement 159

Red Beans and Rice 159

Bringing out the best in others and ourselves 160

Airline puns. 160

Unintended Compliment 161

The Deaf Yorkie 161

The Gentle Bully 162

PT and a Bully 162

Magazine ad 162

A comedian gives it his best shot. 162

Suspicious Politician 162

Big diamond. 163

A Career in Politics 164

Toilet paper color 165

Dating 165

Minimum wage 166

True love? 166

Settling the score. 166

Eskimos 168

Keys locked inside... 168

The Loving Frenchman.. 168

Be sure it's the correct move 169

The most important things 169

Acronyms 171

Q. Sometimes rescuing someone can be illegal 171

The New Brain.. 172

How Canada got its name 172

Punctuation 173

Holiday joke 173

The pill worked too well! 174

Humor and Advertising 175

An old one. We all get older... 175

Donkey race.. 176

Why wait?... 177

Getting even.. 178

George isn't dumb 180

Generous... 180

Answers to Quiz Questions...182

Thank you for choosing this book! 184

About the authors...185

Bruce Miller...185

TeamGolfwell...185

We Want to Hear from You! 186

Other Books by Bruce Miller and Team Golfwell 187

[1] Mayo Clinic Staff, "Stress relief from laughter? It's no joke," https://www.mayoclinic.org/healthy-lifestyle/stress-management/in-depth/stress-relief/art-20044456

[2] Reference.com, "How many times does an average person laugh", https://www.reference.com/science-technology/many-times-average-person-laugh-8f57f06b637760dd

[3] The lawyer portal, https://www.thelawyerportal.com/blog/top-10-weirdest-laws-around-world/

[4] Ibid. https://www.thelawyerportal.com/blog/top-10-weirdest-laws-around-world/

[5] American Courthouse.com. Most Unusual laws in Florida, https://americancourthouse.com/10-most-unusual-laws-in-florida/

[6] Slinky, Wikipedia, https://en.wikipedia.org/wiki/Slinky

[7] Add Cointreau to your Margarita, Forbes, https://www.forbes.com/sites/jeanettehurt/2023/04/24/cointreau-wants-people-to-add-it-to-their-margaritas-this-cinco-de-mayo/

[8] Ibid.

[9] Guinness World Records, Guinness World Records.com, https://www.guinnessworldrecords.com/world-records/358711-longest-title-of-a-book

[10] The lawyer portal. Supra.

[11] Ibid.

[12] Harvard Scientists Say These 5 Things Can Prolong Life, MarketWatch.com, https://www.marketwatch.com/story/harvard-says-these-5-habits-can-prolong-your-life-by-10-years-2018-04-30

[13] Ibid.

[14] Building Self-Control Strength: Practicing Self-Control Leads to Improved Self-Control Performance, NCBI, https://www.ncbi.nlm.nih.gov/pmc/articles/PMC2855143/

[15] Ibid.

[16] Cision PR Newswire, Le Bernardin Named #1 Restaurant In The World By La Liste,

[17] Monowi, Nebraska, Wikipedia, https://en.wikipedia.org/wiki/Monowi,_Nebraska

[18] Ibid.

[19] New Zealand man given ridiculous 99-character name after losing poker bet, Telegraph, https://www.telegraph.co.uk/news/newstopics/howaboutthat/10687002/New-Zealand-man-given-ridiculous-99-character-name-after-losing-poker-bet.html

[20] Robert Wadlow, Wikipedia, https://simple.wikipedia.org/wiki/Robert_Wadlow

[21] The 6 Weirdest Laws in Missouri, The Simon Law Firm, https://simonlawpc.com/the-simon-law-firm-p-c/the-weirdest-law-in-missouri/

[22] Kraft Diner, Wikipedia, https://en.wikipedia.org/wiki/Kraft_Dinner

[23] Golf Jokes & Stories, Facebook, https://www.facebook.com/groups/golfjokesandstories

[24] https://www.amazon.com/Bruce-Miller/e/B096C9SN2R?

[25] https://www.amazon.com/Team-Golfwell/e/B01CFW4EQG?

Made in the USA
Las Vegas, NV
02 December 2024

13165470R10125